Accolades for *A Board Prayer*

This is the best book I've ever read on board governance. Framing his reflections around a prayer, Dan is both deeply spiritual and eminently practical. From a posture of humility and clarity – and based on decades of hard-earned wisdom – he has produced a gem.
Alec Hill
President Emeritus - InterVarsity Christian Fellowship USA

With decades of influential service, Dr. Bolin points us to the most important task of board leadership: prayer. Foundational, diagnostic, strategic, and Spirit-led prayer — the most important task of your service.
April Moreton, Ph.D., CFRE
Vice President for Advancement - Dallas Theological Seminary

A Board Prayer brings clarity of purpose and unity of spirit to the critical work of Christ-centered boards. From firsthand experience of praying **A Board Prayer** in ECFA's boardroom and referring it countless times to the boards of ECFA member organizations, I have been encouraged to see God use this prayer and the principles of this book in powerful ways.
Michael Martin
President & CEO - ECFA

Leadership is always about moving a community toward vibrant health and capacity so they can fulfill their mission. I've always taught that you can't lead a community toward any level of health beyond that of the board, thus making board health a high priority. If you're looking for a tool to contribute to that pursuit of health, this book is exactly what you're looking for.
Richard Dahlstrom
Author, Speaker, Founder - Wilderness Formation Ministries

It is so true that, in Dan's words, "The work of a board is to cultivate the organizational soil so that the ministry can produce a bumper crop of God-honoring fruit." That work is satisfying, sometimes difficult and, most of all, a privilege for anyone engaged in it prayerfully. The role of prayer is essential.
Fred Smith
Founder -The Gathering

A BOARD PRAYER

A BOARD PRAYER

Explore Seven God-Honoring Board Practices

Dr. Dan Bolin

Published by
Refueling in Flight Ministries
Culpeper, Virginia USA
2026

Paperback: 979-8-9850725-7-0
E-book: 979-8-9916464-2-0
Library of Congress Control Number: 2026900629

RIF Publishing
105 N. Main Street, Suite 211
Culpeper, VA 22701
www.refuelinginflight.com

First Edition | Culpeper, VA | 2026

Scripture References
Unless otherwise noted, scripture quotations are taken from The Holy Bible, New International Version®, NIV®. Copyright © 1973, 1978, 1984 by Biblica, Inc. Used with permission of Zondervan. All rights reserved worldwide. www.zondervan.com

Scripture quotations marked ESV are from the ESV® Bible (The Holy Bible, English Standard Version®), © 2001 by Crossway, a publishing ministry of Good News Publishers. Used by permission. All rights reserved.

Names: Bolin, Dan, author. | Pearson, John, foreword by.
Title: A Board Prayer
Subtitle: Explore Seven God-Honoring Board Practices

Dedicated to three board chairs:

John Harper
Brenda Cagle
Lorimer Gray

Whose patience, wisdom, discernment, and encouragement represent the influence of many board colleagues who contributed greatly to my personal development and the foundations of this book.

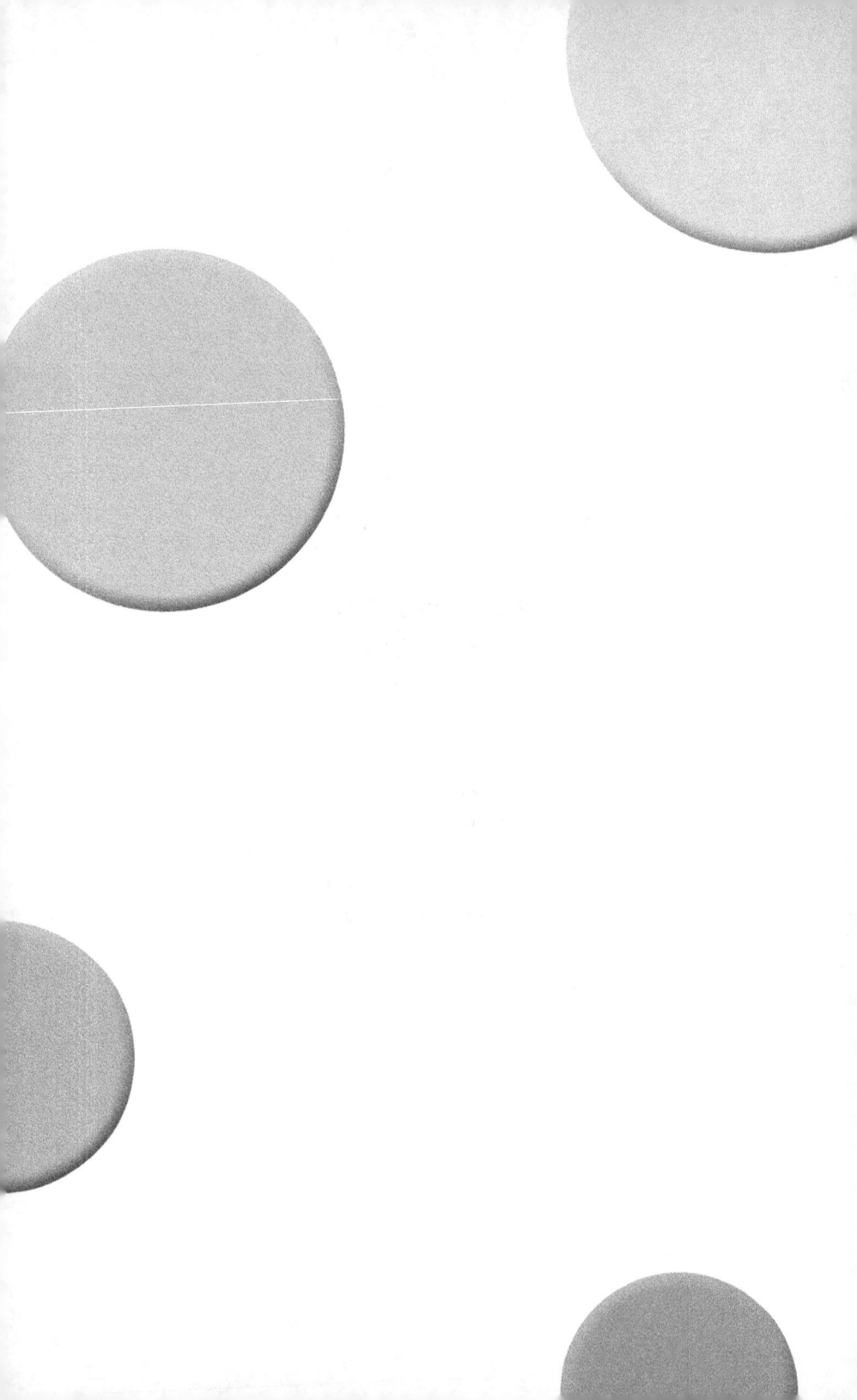

Contents

*Link to free printable version of *A Board Prayer* found in the appendix.

FOREWORD

"Where's the prayer?"

The quarterly board meeting at Seattle's Union Gospel Mission was about to start, and that was the question Linda Ranz, the board chair, asked Jeff Lilley, the president/CEO at the time.

Linda: Jeff, where's the board prayer?

Jeff: What board prayer?

Linda: You know. It's titled *A Board Prayer*, and we read it at the last meeting. You gave copies to every board member, and we went around the board table, each of us reading a sentence out loud. It was powerful! So, where are those copies?

Jeff was confused but enjoying every moment. Of all the issues facing the board at this meeting, his board chair was hyper-focused on prayer!

Linda: Don't you remember? It was so powerful and such a great preamble for doing God's work here, that we agreed to read the prayer at every board meeting!

So they read *A Board Prayer* and were reminded, once again, that issues like reporting, mission clarity, listening, speaking, planning, and unity all require inviting the God of the Universe into the work and relationships of the board.[1]

I've endured more than 500 board meetings over the years (but who's counting?), yet in dozens of boardrooms, I've witnessed those joyful "Aha!" moments when God speaks and board members listen—and respond.

Clearly, the Lord inspired Dan Bolin to write *A Board Prayer.* I've read this remarkable prayer hundreds of times, yet each time the Holy Spirit faithfully elbows me about one or more lines. (*I'm a slow learner!*) I've also seen board members respond to those holy jabs. What fun and what joy!

This is a spiritual no-brainer: read this prayer as you prepare for your next board meeting. Pray this prayer as you begin your board meeting. And as Steve Macchia urges, listen for the *Tap! Tap! Tap!* nudges on your heart from the Holy Spirit.

My most recent nudge from this prayer: "Allow me to focus on what is being said more than how I will respond." *Yikes!*

Board service, as Dan explains, requires both theory and theology. Hopefully, your board members are lifelong learners. John Maxwell wrote, "If you want to lead, you have to learn. If you want to continue to lead, you must continue to learn." Imagine trusting pilots and surgeons who are *not* lifelong learners!

I encourage boards to invest in *10 Minutes for Governance* in every board meeting. Appoint a *Leaders Are Readers Champion* who will facilitate a lifelong learning segment at each meeting. Pick a God-honoring governance book and rotate facilitators. Invest five minutes in summarizing a book and then invite five minutes for Q&A.

---

1   *Dan Busby and John Pearson, "Prioritize Prayer Over Problems: Create space for prayer—serious supplications for a serious work," Lesson 10, in Lessons From the Nonprofit Boardroom: 40 Insights for Better Board Meetings, Second Edition (Winchester, VA: ECFA Press, 2018), 50-51.*

Start with this insightful book. *A Board Prayer* is packed with wisdom, wit, practical takeaways, and the potential for numerous holy moments. You'll highlight Dan's discerning insights. Examples:

- Why you should give Breathe Right® nasal strips to every board member.
- Four things block boards from seeing clearly: success, superficiality, same old - same old, and subterfuge.
- Why a board member was the lone no vote: "If anyone ever reads these minutes, I want them to know that someone was awake."
- The biblical picture of meekness is power under control.
- Wise boards *encourage* discussion, *control* discussion, and *refine* discussion.

I've often mentioned to board members: "There are no dysfunctional organizations—only dysfunctional boards."

Read *A Board Prayer* together and trust God to enrich your board's character, competence, and courage.

By John Pearson
Board Governance Consultant & Author

INTRODUCTION

Board work is always life or death! Board decisions either breathe life into the church or nonprofit organization, or they suck the life out of it. Good boards energize their institutions, while misguided, ignorant, or self-serving boards destroy the soul of their ministry. Board work can be the best part of a church or nonprofit organization or the worst.

I have seen both sides of the coin, and for the most part, boards are filled with noble people trying to do their best. These volunteers contribute deeply to their church or nonprofit ministry and work hard to see them prosper. But not all boards are healthy. Some are populated with troubled people who put their own interests ahead of the welfare of the institution. Boards are reminiscent of the girl in the nursery rhyme,

There was a little girl,
Who had a little curl,
Right in the middle of her forehead,
And when she was good
She was very, very good,
And when she was bad, she was horrid!

I have worked directly for boards for about 40 years. I have interacted with some of the best people on the planet – and a few curmudgeons. I have enjoyed deep and significant relationships with hundreds of board members whom I have served under or alongside. Most were wonderful, a few were miserable, but I learned from all of them.

Shortly after I started my CEO position at Pine Cove, I had a meaningful and memorable conversation with one of my board members, Bob Buford. Bob was just one of several exceptional board members who mentored me through my early, turbulent years. We stood in the driveway of his home and at the end of our talk, he asked a question I will never forget. "What can I do to help you be successful?" What a great question for a seasoned, veteran leader to ask an excited, enthusiastic, inexperienced young director who *didn't know what he didn't know*!

My first impulse was to ask for money. He had it and the camp needed it, but my answer proved much more valuable. I said, "Bob, I'm good at the program side of camp, but I don't know much about the administrative side. Can you teach me something about managing and leading the business part of camp?"

I did not know Bob well enough to read his response. He leaned back against his car and said, "Let me think about that." I went home wondering if I had said the right thing or blown it. Later, as I got to know Bob much better, I realized I had pushed the right button.

Two weeks later I received a packet of information with a stack of reading material and an invitation to attend a training meeting on Tuesday afternoons in Bob's office, for which I cleared my schedule. For the next eight weeks, the leaders of about a dozen local nonprofits and a few government agencies gathered in Bob's conference room where we gleaned wisdom on strategic planning, time management, hiring, staff evaluation, marketing, leadership, and a host of other topics. I still have pages and pages of notes.

Through Bob's founding and involvement with the Leadership Network and the Halftime Movement, his mantra was always, "My fruit grows on other people's trees." Seeing his advice, training, and encouragement multiplied through the influence and impact of many ministries fulfilled his dream.

Guiding an organization while it matures, strengthens, and produces abundant fruit is the challenge all boards face. Except in small, local, or start-up contexts, boards don't do the work. They enable the staff and volunteers to accumulate and utilize limited resources effectively to achieve their desired results. The work of a board is to cultivate the organizational soil so that the ministry can produce a bumper crop of God-honoring fruit.

Tom Landry, the first and longtime coach of the Dallas Cowboys said, "The job of a coach is to make players do what they don't want to do to achieve what they want to achieve." Boards have a coaching responsibility. They help clarify direction, maintain focus, and allocate limited resources. They say *no* to good yet distracting ideas, evaluate programs and people, all to help the institution stay focused on doing well what needs to be done. Effective boards help their organizations avoid distractions and remain attentive to their well-articulated mission. They use resources wisely and overcome the incessant torrent of challenges and opportunities that confront all churches and nonprofit ministries. The goal of *institutional focus* is to enable the church or nonprofit organization to accomplish the great thing God has ordained it to do and produce much fruit.

A copy of the *Prayer*, a link to a printable version, along with the backstory, and ideas of how to benefit from this *Prayer* are listed in the Appendix.

It is my prayer that this book will enable church and nonprofit boards to do God's work in God-honoring ways.

CHAPTER 1

THANK GOD

Dear God,

Thank you for calling this ministry into existence and for allowing it to serve and care for the people you love.

The lady excitedly waved at me from across the room. She looked familiar, but I couldn't place her and certainly could not recall her name. Not wanting to offend, I waved back. The awkward moment took a turn for the worse when another lady from behind rushed past me waving eagerly toward the first.

My assumption that I was the focus of her attention quickly dissolved as I realized I was just the wrong guy in the wrong place. Thinking that the moment was about me led to an awkward and embarrassing experience. I turned and glided out of the room.

Boards are badly mistaken when they think their work is about them. Boards exist to serve their organizations, consider the interest of the many stakeholders connected to the church or ministry, and ultimately to be good stewards of God's resources.

We call them *board meetings*, as well we should. The members of the board gather for information, insights, deliberation, and decisions. However, the purpose of a board meeting is never about the board. The meeting is always about the ministry and the people served, those who benefit from the institution's existence and effectiveness. Maybe these gatherings should be called *beneficiary meetings*.

Going even deeper, the work is God's work, and the people served are God's people. Boards merely steward the institution, aligning the church or nonprofit ministry's limited resources to provide the best possible service to the greatest number of people.

God loves the people served by the ministry, the campers, parishioners, students, patients, hungry, homeless, addicts, artists, scientists, athletes, clients of every stripe. And he loves the *board members* too. In fact, he loves the board enough to entrust the work of caring for his people to them, for better or for worse.

In a sense, these are not *board meetings*, or *beneficiary meetings*, they are *God's meetings*. He calls institutions into being, therefore, boards must perform their responsibilities and exercise their authority in ways that *honor* God and *serve* His people. So, what does the work look like?

The *serve others* part is slightly easier to define and quantify than the *honoring God* part. The *serving others* part means boards establish goals and strive to achieve those objectives. They pray, set plans, make decisions, solve problems, evaluate programs, and supervise the CEO. Boards read reports, review financial documents, discuss threats and opportunities all while sitting under Damocles' Sword, never knowing when the next crisis will befall the institution, but fully aware that when it does, they will bear the brunt of the painful moment.

Boards count inputs and outcomes: volunteer hours, meals served, beds filled, Sunday attendance, offering size, and any number of actions that tend to be measurable. We love to count, and that is not a bad thing, just not the only thing.

What then, does *honor God* look like? How do boards reflect the godly attitudes of *love, joy*, and *peace* in their work? And how do they exude that spiritual breath throughout the entire ministry? It begins by giving as much consideration to *what* is done as to *how* it is accomplished. God expects us to be responsible with the tasks before us, and to be honorable in the ways those tasks are accomplished.

The good work we are called to do should be done through godly means that flow from a heart that desires to honor God and love people, even in the board room.

Whether *board meeting* or *beneficiary meeting*, these are *God's meetings.* So, we must conduct them in ways that honor him and serve his people. Start with an attitude of humility. Eagerly strive to see *God's will done on earth as it is in heaven.* And then do his *will* his *way.*

PRAYERFUL BOARDS

Prayerful boards understand that God's work must be done in God honoring ways.

Thank you for the various perspectives represented in this meeting and the things we will
learn from one another.

A board's greatest strength, and potentially its greatest
Achilles Heel, is *diversity of opinions.* Great power is gained
by sharing perspectives; each of us sees the world a little differently. We can all learn from one another's ideas,
opinions, and viewpoints. Weaving together divergent
strands of thought can create a delightful, variegated tap-
estry. Different backgrounds of gender, age, biblical inter-
pretations, geography, race, and occupation, broaden the
group's collective insights, and increase the value and
effectiveness of board decisions.

Representative boards are made up of members voic-
ing and protecting the interests of a specific constituency.
They add significant complexity to the many challenges
facing boards. The deepest loyalty of representative members tends to reside with the church, city, denomination,
organization, or whatever entity is selecting and sending
the board member. Representative board members generally think about the consequences each decision will have
on their specific group. They ask, "How will this decision
play at home? Will this be good or harmful for my primary
constituency?" Multiple perspectives are crucial to foster lively and beneficial board deliberations. However,
entrenched loyalties to one segment of the institution can
prove detrimental to the good of the entire ministry.

Some may consider the difference between board
perspectives and board *representation* an insignificant
nuance, but the distinction is crucial. Boards exist for the
common good. Therefore, the more that healthy perspectives are expressed within board discussions, the greater
the opportunity for exceptional outcomes. As one ad cam-
paign put it, *Better ingredients, better pizza,* so too, better
inputs, better decisions.

When loyalty to the larger organization is subordinated
by its members' loyalty to their sending constituencies,
the process can become contentious and the decisions

reached are *acceptable* to all, rather than *exceptional* for all. Progress may be thwarted, and decisions brokered to find an outcome that is grudgingly acceptable or tolerable to each of the *sending groups* rather than wrestling with the issue and finding the best possible solution that is beneficial to the *entire institution.*

Multiple perspectives, coalescing to discover an optimal solution, are needed, not myopic representations. Boards benefit when a wide array of viewpoints converge to create the best possible decisions. Boards need the strength and power that comes from listening to the perspectives of others, learning from new insights, widening their knowledge base, and striving to find the best possible outcomes for all.

PRAYERFUL BOARDS

Prayerful boards remember that healthy inputs produce exceptional outcomes.

Thank you for the privilege of corporately receiving reports, and with one voice establishing policies, discovering direction, setting goals, and encouraging those who serve in this ministry.

Boards function as the owner of their church or nonprofit ministry. They make big, significant, long-lasting decisions for their institution. To do that, they need good information. Successful board service begins with sufficient, accurate, and pertinent data. To fulfill their responsibilities and to serve effectively, board members need shared and relevant information. A wise board member once told me, "Give us good information and we will help you make good decisions."

Functioning in the role of the owner, boards must not become schizophrenic. They cannot function as if corporate *multiple-personality disorder* is healthy. Members of the board must agree on policies to live by, pathways to follow, and evaluation processes to apply to people and programs. And then, through prior commitment to the greater good of the ministry, speak with *one voice.*

Once adequate, accurate, and relevant information is in play, what do boards do with it? They use it as the basis for planning and decision making to enhance and grow the church or ministry. Boards work best when they establish policies and then either step aside and expect the staff to work within these limitations. Or switch hats and become volunteers and serve the organization to fulfill those board-approved directives and policies.

So, what is a policy? In its simplest form, a policy is *the answer to a question that will be asked again.* It need not be a highly technical or finely crafted document, just a clear statement that answers a question. Staff members create many operational policies, but the board should establish or approve the more comprehensive, long-lasting, and expensive ones. Boards work best when they set policies that can be applied in all situations by everyone within the organization. Questions arise that need consistent answers, and policies provide that reliable response.

Can my son turn in late homework? Our school's policy on late homework is....

Can our children visit their grandfather in the hospital? Our hospital's policy on child visitors is....

Can my daughter use her cellphone while at camp? Our camp's policy on cellphone use is....

The answers to these questions are policies. They should be simple, clear, and applied consistently.

Whether setting policies, establishing plans, evaluating people and programs, or encouraging the staff, it is critical that the board speaks with *one voice*. Mixed messages, misinformation, and distortions can occur when multiple board members express their opinions or convey their versions of events beyond the board. Dissension and confusion reign when ministry stakeholders apply their versions of board interactions in ways that best suit their interests.

One voice does not mean that differing opinions should not be expressed, quite the contrary, spirited debate is often healthy and helpful. But what *one voice* does mean is that debate, opposing opinions, and candid deliberations stay in the room. Only the mutually agreed outcomes are shared with the broader community of stakeholders. Written statements are preferred when addressing sensitive topics, and the board chair, or a designee, should be the mouthpiece, speaking for the united board.

PRAYERFUL BOARDS

Prayerful boards stay unified and speak clearly with one voice.

Thank you for the many people whose lives will be influenced through our meeting - other board members, staff, volunteers, donors, participants, vendors, and generations yet unborn who will benefit from the decisions we make today.

Boards balance many competing demands. They are called to consider and respect a broad array of differing opinions. The desires of the staff, the wishes of the donors, the needs of the clients, limited resources, unlimited dreams, immediate threats, and the horizon lined with immense opportunities all collide in the boardroom.

Many voices call for help with legitimate requests, and boards must address complex challenges. At times, those tough decisions are functional and utilitarian. Boards ask and respond to questions like, what kind of ministry return can be expected from the investment of time, money, and people? Or is this a reasonable budgetary stretch based on the current economic realities? But at times, the board's way forward is based on more philosophical or ethical questions. Is this the *right* thing to do? Which pathway is the *best*? Who will be *helped* and who will be *hurt*?

The board's job is to make tough corporate decisions. And those decisions impact the hopes, dreams, satisfactions, and livelihoods of many people. Everyone involved loves the ministry and wants to see the work grow and prosper. But they approach their challenges from different directions. Paid staff members engage work differently than volunteers. Donors approach the ministry from one direction while beneficiaries arrive through a separate doorway. Vendors, government agencies, and oversight groups all have their own perspectives. Boards must weigh inputs from all the stakeholders and then determine what is the *best* path forward for the institution.

Possibly the least considered and yet most significant stakeholders are the people of the future. Someday, many years downstream, people's lives will be influenced by the decisions made in the boardroom today. The next generation of parishioners, campers, students, listeners, or patients will have spiritual, physical, emotional, and relational needs that the ministry may someday address. Board decisions must balance the short-term dreams of different sub-groups within the organization, while not impugning the prospect of an even greater and wider ministry impact in the days ahead.

Prayerful boards strive to discover and do what is best for all.

And God, thank you for entrusting your ministry into our care. Help us be worthy of the trust that you and others place in us.

I prefer the word *trustee* over the term *board member*. The word *trustee* speaks to the heart of a board member's role and consistently reminds us of the critical responsibility board members shoulder as guardians who serve the interests of others. They are *trusted* by many constituencies to act in the best interest of all.

Trust is a fragile gift. Actually, trust is not a true gift in the sense that it is transferred from one person to the next; trust is never *given*, it is only *loaned*. When we place our trust in another, we can recall it at any time.

Trust is rarely an *all-in* proposition. We generally put our toe in the relational water and evaluate the trustworthiness of the person across from us. Those who are faithful with little, are likely to be faithful with much. And so, trust grows.

Trust is the complex mortar that bonds leaders and followers. At least four ingredients coalesce to foster the development of trust: *character, competence, shared emotional experiences, and transparency.* As to *character*, trust grows in the fertile soil of fairness, honesty, and integrity. Considering *competency*, people trust those who know what they are doing as they steward valuable resources and meet significant deadlines. *Shared emotional experiences*, painful or joyful, accelerate the growth of trust. People bond deeply and rapidly in the peaks and valleys of life, and board experiences are filled with splendid mountaintops and dark ravines. *Transparency* is critical because trust prospers when information is shared to the highest degree possible, and issues are discussed in the broadest acceptable forum.

Boards that are serious about building trust throughout their institutions must demonstrate corporate character and competence while connecting warmly and openly.

Boards can never force their clients, donors, volunteers, or staff members to trust them, they can only *be trustworthy*. Demonstrating trustworthiness is *job one* for board members. The trustworthiness of any board will determine the degree of confidence or caution it enjoys with constituents, staff, donors, vendors, volunteers, and sister institutions.

Some board members think they hold positions of power. In reality, when churches and nonprofit ministries are involved, power resides with the followers. In a healthy, non-coercive relationship, power is held by the one extending trust. Followers control trust while boards and the organization's leaders can only act in a trustworthy manner. In a free and voluntary system, followers control the decision to extend or withdraw trust. Staff members stay long-term or move elsewhere. Volunteers recommit or find other opportunities in which to invest their discretionary time. Donors provide vital funds, or they entrust their stewardship dollars to other organizations. Parishioners, students, campers, listeners, patients, and all other fee-based clients, are the ones who choose where to go to school or camp, what station to listen to, or where to seek help.

Boards cannot force followers to follow, they can only be trustworthy. The more trustworthy they are, the more likely it is that people will follow. The challenge of every board is to demonstrate competence, exhibit godly character, share healthy emotional moments, and be transparent. The greater the board's trustworthiness, the higher the prospect of a healthy degree of institutional trust.

Prayerful boards strive to be trustworthy.

Personal Reflections

Are you thankful for the opportunity to serve on this board or is it a nuisance?

What unique perspectives do you bring to board discussions?

How committed are you to supporting the board's one-voice policy?

Do others on the board trust you more today than they did one year ago?

Board Discussion

⬤ *For what is this board grateful? Make a list.*

⬤ *What decisions will the board make in coming months that could impact the grandchildren of the current beneficiaries?*

⬤ *What are some things the board could do to enhance the trust of the staff and those served?*

⬤ *What are some perspectives the board should add to provide additional input for better planning and decision making?*

CHAPTER 2

REPORT HONESTLY

Father, allow me to report honestly.

As a schoolboy I spent my summers picking berries and beans from the fertile farmland outside Portland, Oregon. The season started with strawberries, migrated to raspberries, and then into blackberries. The last few weeks before school started were all about string beans. Berries I loved. I could pick a while and then enjoy a few handfuls of fresh, plump, luscious, sweet, Oregon berries. Unfortunately, there is no immediate gratification with beans.

During the bean harvest, we received three cents a pound for every gunnysack we filled. The goal was to fill each bag with at least 34 pounds of beans to ensure earning at least one dollar per bag. It did not take long to develop a keen awareness of the weight of each bag. Strategies emerged to *augment* a 32-pound bag into a 34-pounder. Occasionally, a stick, rock, tin can, or dirt clod hidden in the bottom of the bag made the difference. I had *friends* who actually did such things!

We all want to appear bigger and better than we truly are. We want to portray ourselves with a little more power, wisdom, importance, and confidence than we actually have. We also want to hide our shortcomings while accentuating the things that make us look good and help us appear more valuable. Staff reports, committee presentations, board updates, and year-end donor statements can stretch the truth and feed our desire to look a little bit bigger than we are. We strive to hide our weaknesses and limitations, but deep inside we know the truth.

Individuals exaggerate. We chalk that up to human nature, but the practice of puffing reports can also permeate institutions. Good board work begins with accurate information and honest representation. Trustworthy data is important for board deliberations and crucial to build the confidence of a watching world. Authentic presentations, especially in the hard areas of missteps and failures, are important to the clients we serve, the donors and stakeholders who have a vested interest in our ministry, and those a few steps removed who peek into our practices. Ultimately, authenticity is critical for our staff members, and ourselves, because it is the right thing to do.

We would all like to be seen as a bigger bag of beans, a little smarter, a little wiser, a little more competent, and a little more successful. But what we truly need is to be a little more truthful. Telling the truth about our competency, or lack thereof, provides significant insight into our character. We need to strengthen our character while developing our competency as we strive to function well individually, as corporate boards, and as followers of Christ.

Prayerful boards know that honesty is always the best policy.

Help me tell the whole truth, not just the parts that make me look good.

Good decisions flow from good information. Accurate reporting not only allows us to sleep well at night knowing that we have not presented a *false witness*. Truthfulness also ensures that we have provided accurate information upon which we can form good decisions. Doing the right thing and telling the whole story lay the groundwork for wise decisions.

I served on the board of a wonderful ministry that spent most of its meetings listening to excellent and informative Bible studies. The leader was a great Bible teacher, and the meetings revolved around what he did best. Who wants to argue against Bible study? That was fine, until we discovered we had no money to pay the bills and meet our debt obligations. Nothing he said was untrue. Everything he told us was biblical. But it was all a smokescreen to obscure the rough and tough issues that he lacked the courage to confront.

Too often I'm tempted to focus on the statistics that show progress toward a significant goal, tell a story that presents me as the hero, or read the letter that sings my praises. I tend to cherry pick the details that make me and what I do look just a little bit better than I know I am.

Downstream, those misrepresentations not only erode the effectiveness of the board in making well-informed decisions. Those half-truths also weaken our corporate character and atrophy our institutional souls.

Prayerful boards search for the whole truth and nothing but the truth.

Let me not bury bad news in mounds of data and detail, and don't let me gloss over painful issues or personal failures.

The Bible is full of stories built around hiding and deceit – and they generally do not end well. Adam and Eve sinned and *hid* from God. Achan stole silver, gold, and valuable clothing from Jericho and *hid* them in his tent. Jonah fled to a ship trying to *hide* from God. The One-Talent Servant *went off and hid* his treasure. In the face of painful or embarrassing news, our natural tendency is to hide.

Hiding is especially true of bad corporate news because the failure, shortcoming, or error mushrooms as it becomes public. Mistakes within the confines of our private lives are less noticeable. Only our families and a few close friends see our failures and view our weaknesses. But corporately, in the public eye, where we stand cold and naked with the spotlight shining on our incompetence, failure, or negligence, we learn to hide.

The self-deception of human nature lures us into thinking the safest strategy in times of trouble, is hiding. But actually, hiding is the place of greatest danger. The fresh air of open authenticity provides the cathartic healing we all need. It allows others to come alongside and share their strengths to supplement our weakness. Their experience, wisdom, and support cover our naïveté and errors.

No one is omnicompetent (a word introduced to me by Bryon Loritts). We all need each other. I cannot recall a time when I asked for help unscrambling a leadership or management egg, that other board members were not willing to offer wisdom and support. We fear that people will think less of us if we expose our weaknesses. Ironically, most people think more highly of us when we come clean and ask for help.

The root problem is that our personal identity aligns too closely with the institution's identity. The success or failure of the church or organization becomes our personal success or failure. The victories and defeats of the ministry become our own victories and defeats. This erroneous perspective leads to three critical implications:

First, we forget that we are stewards, trustees using our gifts to serve our Master. This is not our ministry. God expects us to be good stewards and to work diligently. But the church or nonprofit ministry is his - not ours.

Second, we bear a burden we were never intended to carry. God calls us to be faithful, not necessarily successful, at least in the ways the world measures success. Faithful servants do all they can to achieve their objectives and accomplish their goals. They work within the complex dynamic of family, health, friendships, and rest - and then they sleep at night.

Third, and possibly the most unforgiving error is, *we forget that our true identity flows from our relationship with God* - not the success or failure of our ministry. Successful leaders embody their institution's values and to the outside world they can become Mr. or Ms. _____ (insert name of institution). But that is different from an unhealthy confusion between what God sets before us to *do* and who God calls us to *be*. Our tendency is to sacrifice the private areas of our lives. Our marriage, children, health, and friendships find themselves on the altar of our public persona. We too often barter away the gold of *being good* for the baubles of *looking good*. We tear down *little barns* of family, health, and godliness while striving relentlessly toward the construction of the *bigger barn* of church growth or ministry success.

PRAYERFUL BOARDS

Prayerful boards tell the truth, accept responsibility, learn from criticism, and ask for help.

Help me give credit to others and take responsibility for failure and lack of progress.

During one of my earliest board meetings, as a young CEO, I reported a legitimate and significant success within the ministry. As several members of the board showered praise and appreciation on me, I quickly deflected some of the compliments to the team that had worked diligently and effectively on the project. One wise, clever, and seasoned board member leaned across the table, grinned broadly, and with a twinkle in his eye said, "Son, you need to take the credit, because we will give you the blame." That's the way it is; pastors and CEOs get too much credit for institutional successes, and the blame lands on them when the wheels come off.

In reality, pastors and CEOs don't accomplish much without great teams of staff members and volunteers. Sharing credit with those who do the hard, routine, behind-the-scenes work and honoring those who contribute to the institution's success goes a long way to build trust and establish a healthy working environment. When church and ministry leaders accept responsibility, own their mistakes, and do not assign blame, they build trust and cooperation throughout the institution.

At times, CEOs, board members, and committee leaders enjoy the privilege of sharing good news and successes. At other times they explain institutional and personal missteps and failures. Wise, strong, and godly leaders share the credit for ministry's success with significant contributors and absorb the blame personally.

Most people, deep down inside, want to live lives that demonstrate Romans 12:15. They know that as a ministry family they must *rejoice with those who rejoice, and mourn with those who mourn.* Sharing credit and accepting responsibility are the first two steps for any institution to *rejoice* and *mourn* in healthy ways. Sharing credit and absorbing blame honors God and leads to greater personal and institutional health.

Prayerful boards share credit and accept blame.

Don't let me trivialize serious issues or magnify minor successes.

One way to hide unpleasant or humiliating information is through proportions. We can cleverly allocate an abundance of time for innocuous reporting, thus limiting the opportunity for the board to dig into programs that are off the rails, examine tough staff issues, or drill into the worrisome numbers. Relevancy matters! Boring deeply into superficial accomplishments while blowing past serious concerns can be a highly effective method of hiding problems - *for a while.*

I served on the board of a ministry that operated more than a thousand miles from my home. I was in the area on business, so I added a day to my trip to see the ministry in operation. The director showed me around the facility, and we observed several people benefiting from the services it provided. Then he took me out to lunch. All afternoon he showed me the interesting tourist sites in the area. That evening we went out for another nice meal before calling it a day. I thought it odd that we spent so little time on the grounds of the ministry, and that we did not eat with or have much interaction with the staff or clients. I would have preferred to stay on site the whole time, meet the key personnel, and see more of the work in action. At the same time, I was thrilled to get one-on-one time with a man I admired greatly.

A few months later, the lid blew off. Intense staff conflicts, serious money problems, and major ethical questions all came to the forefront. I saw the ministry, but only briefly. My schedule ensured that I was isolated from discouraged and angry staff members. My distraction kept me from asking too many questions. Nothing said or done was untrue, but the entire experience provided a ruse to hide the painful truth.

Prayerful boards commit major time to major concerns.

L et me tell stories and provide statistics that represent accurately.

Jesus was a master storyteller. He used stories to connect with people, share deep truths, hide insights from his enemies, and clarify murky subjects, and we should do the same. Stories give life to the business-like work of board meetings. Hearing about changed lives and learning about God's life transforming power can energize the functional board responsibilities that too often become challenging and tedious. Charts, graphs, and statistics provide fresh perspectives and establish visual vantage points from which to peer into the numerical jungle.

Stories and statistics are extremely valuable when used with authenticity. But they are also susceptible to misuse, inaccuracy, and subterfuge. Mark Twain's old saying is never more true than in board meetings, "Figures don't lie, but liars figure."

Several decades ago, I enjoyed the humor and wisdom of the *Wittenburg Door*. When the sometimes irreverent yet often insightful magazine arrived, I turned first to the *Letters to the Editor* section. Instead of printing comments of praise and adulation, they printed their *hate mail*. Their honesty and openness to share unfiltered comments like, "Your recent article was heresy." "This is trash, take me off your mailing list," was refreshing as well as humorous. Like jujitsu, a successful defense came by redirecting the force of the attack.

Stories and statistics provide windows into the institution. Windows can be crystal clear, providing an accurate view of the operational details and realistic outcomes of the church or ministry. But windows can also be dirty, smudged, or cracked, distorting the image of whatever is behind them. Only a commitment to integrity and authenticity can ensure that the windows the boards peer through will open accurate insights into the heart of the church or institution.

When stories and statistics describe the institution's strengths *AND* weaknesses, it creates a context of authenticity and transparency where trust develops rapidly, and where boards do their best work.

PRAYERFUL BOARDS

Prayerful boards use authenticity to establish and grow trust.

H elp me remember that good information provides a smooth pathway to good decisions.

A colleague, with whom I served alongside on a national board, always encouraged us to, "Tell 110% of the bad news." Boards need to know the threats, perils, problems, and concerns their institutions face, and they need to learn about these challenges while they are still manageable. Like fire, simmering problems and troubling trendlines can be contained and addressed when small. The ones that grow unchecked are the ones that do the greatest damage.

Good plans built on faulty assumptions are never effective. A well-built house, constructed upon an uneven foundation, will never be square. The windows will stick, wallpaper will not align, and the doors will not shut properly. Like the house Jesus described in Matthew 7:26-27, organizational strength begins with a solid foundation. Accurate information allows boards, pastors and CEOs to build their ministry upon a reliable base.

One sure way to impede the flow of adequate, accurate, and relevant information is to *shoot the messenger*. People who bring bad news, or share corporate deficiencies, need to be commended, not excoriated. When people are punished for telling the truth, they will soon leave, learn to say nothing, or voice only what the leadership wants to hear.

Boards need good information and adequate opportunity to analyze and dissect data. To do that, boards need to create an environment that honors truth-telling. Establishing openness does not begin during a crisis. One practice that sets the tone is an uncomplicated *high and low* reporting process. Simply ask the question, "Since the last time we met, what is the best thing that has happened within the organization and what is the worst?" Generally, the positive reports are very encouraging, and the negative revelations are rather manageable. But sometimes, that question creates the doorway through which critically important information related to dangerous trends or threatening circumstances comes to the forefront of the board's collective awareness.

Circumstances change. What is a strength one year may be a weakness the next. Do not rely on old data to make today's decisions. The recent past is the best predictor of the future. Stay relevant, keep current, and encourage the free flow of information. Board decisions are never better than the data used in the discernment process.

PRAYERFUL BOARDS

Prayerful boards use good information
to make good decisions.

Personal Reflections

Can you recall a time when you enhanced a report to make you or the institution appear better or more successful than it truly was?

What are some ways you have shared credit in the past to include and encourage staff, volunteers, or donors?

What are some helpful ways you might respond to negative or painful corporate information?

Can you recall a time when you failed to share bad, negative, or painful information? How did you feel about this omission?

Board Discussion

What are some ways the board can encourage greater honesty in reporting?

What can we do to identify areas of weakness so that we can fix problems without assessing unwarranted blame?

Are there ever times when telling truth to the board is unwise or unhealthy?

When was the last time a mistake was owned before the board? Has that been too long?

CHAPTER 3

SEE CLEARLY

G od, as we approach this meeting, help us see clearly.

My friend the eye doctor told me I would see him professionally when I turned forty. I was quite proud when the birthday came and went, and I still enjoyed 20/20 vision. A few years later, standing in a mountain stream attempting to tie a fly to my tippet, I realized the time had come to see the eye doctor. When we can't see clearly, everything becomes more challenging. Our vision and our effectiveness go hand in hand.

Renowned businessman and author Max De Pree said, "The first job of leadership is to define reality." If he is correct, then the number one job of any board is to *see clearly*.

We all tend to view our world with distorted vision, we see what we want to see. Either we overlook the painful and threatening realities surrounding us, or we see distress and disaster lurking around every corner. This human tendency toward distorted vision can be mitigated or multiplied during board deliberations. Boards must strive to see themselves, their institutions, and the world in which they operate with 20/20 vision.

The board's clarity should be directed *internally*, *externally*, and *futuristically*. First, like a *microscope*, boards must look deeply into the soul of their organizations, examining details and exploring data. They need to honestly assess the internal operations as well as the deep-seated corporate attitudes and values that influence the decisions and direction of the church or nonprofit ministry. At times, an objective external assessment is necessary. A board may need a neutral third-party to hold up the cold mirror of reality, to reveal a painful unseen fact.

Second, like a *periscope*, the board's vision must scan the broadest reaches of the community it serves and survey the legal, cultural, demographic, economic, and religious contexts within which it operates. Communities change. Contexts ebb and flow. Needs increase or decrease. Values morph. The speed of change is accelerating, therefore, more and more, boards need to stay in touch with the shifting realities that control the ministry's context.

Third, like a *telescope*, boards must probe the farthest reaches of the future, looking as far down the road as possible. Some of the decisions made today will ripple through many decades and impact generations to come. Wise boards open doors for future ministry opportunities and are cautious when closing doors that may restrict future growth.

Four things block boards from seeing clearly: *success, superficiality, same old - same old*, and *subterfuge*.

Success is wonderful but also perilous. Victories allow leaders to become satisfied and sloppy. The attitude of, *if it ain't broke don't fix it*, can reign supreme. Financial success often provides the abundance that allows churches and ministries to say *yes* to distracting opportunities. Abundance creates margins that lead to relaxed evaluations of people and programs. Success should be celebrated; it is a good thing. But boards should not become lax in fulfilling their key responsibilities of planning, evaluating, and stewarding resources. Especially during the good times, boards should keep their eyes on the mission and intently focus on the leverage points that provide ministry effectiveness.

Superficial examinations are never enough. I'm always intrigued by the game that sets two similar pictures side-by-side. At first glance, they look identical but upon further study, subtle differences emerged between the two pictures. Boards must ask themselves: "What has changed? What is different? What slight alteration seems to be hidden in the details?" Organizations change. A superficial glance is never enough. Over time, subtle differences can mutate in the shadows of unexamined details. Many organizational changes are innocuous, just tactical alterations to programs or systems, but some are significant and strategic. If unnoticed for too long, these modifications can aggregate into significant changes. Boards should look deeply into the numbers, systems, and practices of the organization. They also examine closely the cultural, demographic, economic, religious, and legal shifts in the world around them.

Same old - same old can rock any board to sleep. Following well-worn routines and established patterns has value. Proven practices provide stability and security and afford the opportunity for steady improvement. However, monotony can mesmerize well-meaning board members, keeping them from engaging enthusiastically with data in fresh and meaningful ways. Creative approaches to meetings can help boards see more clearly. Routines need a shake-up every now and then. New settings, new styles of reporting, new methods of interacting, and new consultants are just some ways to wipe away the corporate cobwebs.

Subterfuge is rare, but deadly. Boards must have confidence that the numbers they are working with are legitimate. An annual financial audit is always wise. An outside, objective set of qualified eyes helps the church or ministry avoid ethical nightmares and ensures the wise and appropriate use of resources. Reviews of programs and internal operating systems are also important. The eyes of a trained, objective outsider will give confidence to the board members that they are making decisions based upon accurate and trustworthy information.

Prayerful boards ask God for eyes to see internally, externally, and futuristically.

H elp us see the issues before us from many perspectives – but ultimately from your perspective. Align our thoughts with your thoughts and our work with your desire.

The beauty of a board that brings multiple perspectives into its deliberations is that the degree of magnification increases many times over. The lenses of geography, age, gender, theology, occupation, race, and more provide greater clarity of vision for the task ahead.

Even though planning involves thinking about big, beautiful, and better futures, boards should begin with an awareness of corporate limits. There is only so much that any institution can see and do. God speaks through his prophet Isaiah and reminds us, *As the heavens are higher than the earth, so are my ways higher than your ways and my thoughts than your thoughts* (Isaiah 55:9). God has no limits – but we do. Stretching is important and can be exciting, but enthusiasm should always be tempered with a healthy dose of reality. An awareness of our human limits and reflection on God's recent leading provide insight into the direction he might have for the church or nonprofit ministry in the days to come.

Boards must ensure that acts of service to the King are done in ways that honor the King. Both the *what* of ministry, and the *way* of ministry should align with the values God commends. As a board investigates the effectiveness of its church or nonprofit ministry, *what should it look for*? Positive cash flow? Sure. Increasing donor support? Fabulous. Growing attendance/participation? Great. Expanding volunteer support? Wonderful. The answers to these questions provide a peek into the health of the institution. But what about the *way* ministry activity is performed? Is the organization accomplishing the thing(s) it feels called to do, while expressing attitudes and demonstrating values that honor God?

I've engaged in numerous discussions concerning the board and/or staff's roles in strategic planning. Who initiates the process? Who responds and refines ideas? Where does the process begin? I believe we start on stronger theological footing and apply a healthier process when we abandon *vision casting* and approach the challenge as *vision discovery*. Is it *our will* that is being done or *God's will*? Is it *our kingdom* that we long for, or *His*?

As boards deliberate, they must be mindful that their role is to *discern* the will of God. Ultimately, a board's succeeds to the degree that it aligns the *actions* and *attitudes* of the institution with the will of God.

*Prayerful boards seek God's will and do
God's will in God-honoring ways.*

G od, help us see our ministry's strengths and weaknesses and embrace both.

We have already encountered the fallacy of *omnicompetence*. No one is the perfect manager or leader, we all have strengths and weaknesses. Each of us experiences moments when we make contributions to our churches or nonprofits and times when we depend upon the skills, abilities, and experiences of others. None of us can do it all.

I found myself in a wonderful small cohort while working on my MBA. Every Monday night for almost two years, Liz, Peggy, Mike, and I ate dinner together comparing notes. Then we spent a couple of hours in class and met afterward to divvy up the assignments. The rest of the week we did our part to contribute to the success of our entire group. I chimed in during courses on leadership, organizational behavior, and marketing. I was not too big of a drag in economics and finance, but when it came to quantitative decision analysis, I needed massive assistance. Liz, Peggy, and Mike carried me all the way to the finish line.

The university I attended designed the program to reflect *real world* conditions. The dean explained that our ability to work in teams would prepare us well for our future leadership opportunities. Helping us learn how to draw on the support of others was a significant focus of their educational design.

Understanding our strengths and admitting our weaknesses is critical on a personal level, and it is also necessary in the board and corporate arenas. All ministries have corporate competencies, things they do well. They also have gaps in their proficiencies that can lead to errors, generate frustration, and prove troubling.

Authenticity and transparency require that boards identify the institution's strengths and weaknesses. Boards must honestly *explore* blind spots. Asking questions, enlisting consultants, conducting interviews, and listening well all provide windows into the reality of the situation. Like mirrors, theses practices allow boards to see themselves clearly.

Once the church or nonprofit identifies its highly effective aspects, capitalizing upon those strengths will produce greater fruitfulness. Doing more and more of what works well is the easiest way to grow, expand, and impact more people. Focusing on existing core competencies allows the ministry to pick low-hanging fruit.

Churches and nonprofits must work to *eliminate* weaknesses within the organization. They should examine systems, facilities, programs, and staff. More often than not, weaknesses boil down to *people*. Be honest and objective in the assessment process and when weaknesses are discovered, follow the age-old, three-fold prescription for improvement:

- *Training* – Does the person just need help understanding what is expected and how to fulfill the job requirements?
- *Transfer* – Does this person need re-potting in a new place within the organization where his or her gifts will be more effective?
- *Termination* – Is it time for a major, and possibly painful change? A new start elsewhere is, at times, the best path forward for everyone.

Look honestly at who you are as an institution and identify the corporate highs and lows. Capitalize on the strengths and mitigate your weaknesses.

Prayerful boards recognize their organizational strengths and weaknesses.

Help us connect the dots between the many good ideas to find the great idea you have for us.

Great ideas rarely hatch fully grown. They emerge in messy, immature, fragile, yet hopeful forms. Abram had a good idea. His faithful servant, Eleazar of Damascus, would someday inherit his vast estate. Abram had no children, no heir to assume control of his immense flocks and fortune, so, why not leave it to his confidant, Eleazar?

Setting his house in order was a good idea, but Abram's plan was not the best path forward. As always, God had a better idea. The decision to establish a seamless transition of wealth and authority was noble and wise. But his grand idea needed refinement, and that occurred when God showed up. Yes, God's promise of a son to Abram changed everything. Additional, reliable, and godly information took a good idea and made it great. The revised plan redirected Abram to a pathway that would change the course of history. (*See Genesis 15:1-6.*)

Some ideas are just bad, they need to be nipped in the bud. But there are many *good* ideas that could be *great* if given serious refinement.

Too often, board members see one flaw in a new idea and dismiss the complete thought. That single weakness becomes the fatal flaw for the entire concept. With one swipe of criticism, a board may miss a potentially valuable contribution. Greater thought, deeper study, and considerable refinement may help the idea blossom into a powerful and significant ministry initiative.

Sometimes new ideas need more than a little refinement, but the related discussion generates synergy that opens new thoughts about greater possibilities. Sometimes the flashlight's beam only shines a few steps ahead, but that progress allows us to see the clear path that lies just out of sight.

Try this exercise. Divide your board into groups of three or four members and give each group $10,000,000 of play money. Ask them how they would use a large, unexpected gift to make the ministry more productive. After their decisions crystallize, have them share those dreams with the entire board. Next, give each group a real, crisp $100 bill. Ask each group what they would do with $100 to make the ministry more effective. A new sign, fixed drinking fountain, shampooed carpet, pizza lunch for the office staff, or many other ideas can emerge. Then make sure you use the money to do what they recommend. Explore how the $100 ideas align with the $10,000,000 dreams. The process will create a safe place for new ideas to emerge, undergo refinement, and potentially enhance the ministry's effectiveness.

Great ideas often need time to mature. Keep the chicks in the nest a while and allow the fledgling ideas to find their wings. Over time, ad hoc study groups, working committees, outside consultants, and research groups may connect the ill-defined dots of a new idea to discover powerful and transformational pathways the Lord has in store for the ministry.

Prayerful boards explore new ideas and
allow them to develop.

Help us distinguish what is significant from what is superficial, what is short-term from what is long-term, and what is best for me from what is best for all.

Early in the Book of Acts, the church leaders faced a monumental crisis.

> *In those days when the number of disciples was increasing, the Grecian Jews among them complained against the Hebraic Jews because their widows were being overlooked in the daily distribution of food. So the Twelve gathered all the disciples together and said, "It would not be right for us to neglect the ministry of the word of God in order to wait on tables. Brothers, choose seven men from among you who are known to be full of the Spirit and wisdom. We will turn this responsibility over to them and will give our attention to prayer and the ministry of the word.* (Acts 6:1-4)

The perilous challenge facing the young church in Jerusalem was actually a double-edged sword. *First* was the threat of *division*, and the flashpoint of this controversy was the favoritism shown during the allocation of their limited food supply. The church provided meals to the poor of their congregation, but with the church's rapid growth, demand outstripped supply. The local Hebraic Jews took care of their own families and friends first, any leftovers went to the newcomers. The Grecian Jews were the newbies. They were fine to have around, until they started consuming the limited resources of the young church.

The *second* threat was *distraction*. The apostles were committed to prayer and the Word of God. They understood their two-fold calling: to connect with God through prayer and to study and proclaim God's word. Dealing directly with the problem of food distribution would have siphoned away time and energy needed to perform their core responsibility.

Bickering about food was not on the disciples' to-do list, but they could see the potentially destructive nature of this tension. Either problem, *division* or *distraction*, could have severely damaged the growth and vitality of the early church.

What to do?

As wise leaders, they applied several universal principles that God designed to foster smooth and effective human relationships. These principles have been used so well by the business community that we think of them as *business principles* – but they apply equally well in business, church, school, nonprofit, and government contexts. These are *not business principles* applied to other contexts, rather they are *universal life principles* that businesses have used well. Sadly, many churches and nonprofit organizations have neglected these principles – and suffered the consequences. Any institution that wants to grow and function in a healthy manner should implement these simple yet significant organizational truths and reap the benefits.

Let's explore some of these time-honored principles that the early Church employed, and that boards today may apply to their churches or nonprofit ministries to keep them effective, focused, sustainable, and operating justly.

MISSION CLARITY

The Apostles concentrated on what they were called to do: pray and preach. They were profoundly committed to these two core activities and would not allow anything to distract them from their high calling. They believed the maxim, first things first, second things not at all. They understood the danger of the problem they faced and committed themselves to seeing that food was distributed equitably – but not by them. They engaged additional people and applied other principles.

COMMUNICATION

No one brokered a backroom deal, there were no anteroom discussions, and no notes slipped under the table. *And the twelve summoned the full number of disciples.* Open and honest discussion, with all the stakeholders, addressed the problem head-on. Because of their transparent communication, some have said the outcome of their congregational meeting was the greatest miracle in the Bible, *And the proposal pleased the whole group!* (Acts 6:5).

JOB PROFILES

Before anyone was considered for a role in resolving this problem, the Apostles clarified the requirements that each member of the group would need to possess to serve in this challenging capacity. *First*, they consider only those displaying spiritual maturity – *full of the Spirit*. And *second*, they needed experience – *and wisdom*. The Apostles clearly articulated what they needed to see demonstrated in the lives of the people they would recruit to fill these important positions.

DELEGATION

Seven well-qualified people were selected to resolve the problem. Interestingly, the name of all seven have Greek, not Hebrew origins. These Seven represented the minority group and had a significant stake in the outcome. We do not know what they did, but they went to work and found a solution. The Apostles deputized the Seven to address this clearly defined problem. They turned the work over to the small task force and then got out of the way.

EMPOWERMENT

The Apostles let the Seven know that the work was significant. They helped the whole community understand the gravitas of this responsibility. The Apostles also reminded themselves of how momentous this task would be and how much trust they were investing in the Seven. The vitality of the young church hung on the success of this group. So, the Apostles empowered them for the work ahead. They *laid their hands on them and prayed over them*. The Apostles did what they did best. They prayed and supported the Seven as this new task-force forged ahead!

Boards must stay focused on the most significant issues, look deep inside, survey the surrounding ministry context, and explore the broadest horizon. To do that, boards need to articulate the institutional purpose and clarify its role within that statement. From its unique vantage point, the board is called to peer beyond the day-to-day challenges and view the opportunities and threats that exist *inside* and *outside* the ministry. And they must ensure that the church or nonprofit considers the needs and interests of each group to build unity and wisely address potential divisions.

PRAYERFUL BOARDS

Prayerful boards identify their desired outcomes and then stay unified and focused.

Personal Reflections

⬤ *What do you think is your greatest contribution, internal analysis, external observations, or future visioning?*

⬤ *Can you remember a time when you and the board did God's work but not in a God-honoring way?*

⬤ *Can you recall a time when your support helped reshape an ill-conceived idea into a great one?*

⬤ *What about your church or ministry do you now see differently than you did before you joined the board?*

Board Discussion

What attitude may threaten your board in the days ahead: success, superficiality, same old – same old, or subterfuge? Why?

What can your board do to become more effective at doing God's work? And what can your board do to become better at doing God's work in God-honoring ways?

What do you consider this church or ministry's three greatest strengths and one greatest weakness?

Do you consider the greatest threat to your ministry's success division or distraction? Or something else?

CHAPTER 4

LISTEN OBJECTIVELY

Help me listen objectively.

My hearing had diminished significantly, and my doctor recommended hearing aids. After a few tests and evaluations, I ordered the devices and prepared to reenter the world of conversations!

As I walked out of my office, I encountered two very nice ladies who worked in my building. "Well, I'm going to get hearing aids," I said.

"Oh, that's *horrible*," said one of the normally encouraging and gracious ladies.

I was taken back, "There's nothing horrible about hearing aids," I retorted.

"No! No!" She shrieked. "I said, that's *adorable!*"

We all laughed, and I said, "That's why I'm getting hearing aids!"

Problems with our hearing and communicating go far beyond our need for hearing aids. We often hear and process information in ways that benefit us and align with our presuppositions.

We tend to filter new information through our preconceived notions and the biases we tenaciously protect. We generally cheer ideas that support our comfortably held positions and look for ways to refute information that contradicts or challenges our suppositions. We listen to new ideas, not so much to learn, but to prepare a defense of the beliefs we grip so tightly.

Good listeners make *great* board members. They are eager to learn, open to new suggestions, ready to gain fresh insights, and understand they do not have all the answers. Similarly, poor listeners tend to cause havoc in the boardroom. Not only do they fail to learn from others, but they also insist on promoting their agendas, arguing fiercely for their positions, and seeing every issue as a win or lose contest. As the old saying goes, "When you don't know what you don't know, you think you know everything."

Issues vary in significance. Sometimes board discussions are rather perfunctory and the consequences of missing a fine nuance of an obscure point may be inconsequential. However, listening should be focused and intense when crucial, irreversible, and long-term issues are in play.

Not everyone is gifted with exceptional listening skills, but fortunately, all of us can learn to listen. One way to improve is to ask mental questions to stay engaged.

- What do I agree with in this presentation? And what do I reject?

- What modifications would improve the idea?
- What might happen if this idea went forward without much change?
- Whose creative genius might add to the discussion?

Another method to enhance one's quality of listening is to look for congruency between what the speaker is saying and their body language, tone of voice, and facial expressions. Is the person's verbal message aligned with the external non-verbal cues?

An additional practice is to restate the message in your own words. Sometimes out loud and publicly, we ask, "What I'm hearing is . . . . Is that accurate?" But more often in the quiet recesses of our own minds we restate the major points and grapple with the rationale for their adoption. Internal clarification forces us to listen effectively.

Good board members listen well and continue to acquire the listening skills needed to become more engaged and better informed.

Prayerful boards consist of people who value learning and who listen objectively.

Allow me the grace to filter angry words and hear the truth behind what is being said.

Listening occurs simultaneously on several levels. First, we listen to the words and take them at face-value. Words have meaning. Therefore, we must accept simple declarative statements for what the words say. Gathering pertinent details and understanding significant arguments is essential if we are to judge information wisely. When we answer the fundamental questions of who, what, when, and where we gain the basic knowledge of the subject.

Second, equally if not more important, is listening for the intensity and emotions generating the message. We intuitively recognize that the words convey more than the simple content. To what degree is the speaker emotionally vested in the proposal? What emotions energize the message: hope, enthusiasm, fear, anger, or some other deep-seated feeling? Is the presentation engaging me affectively as I absorb the content and listen below the surface?

And *third*, we should always look for the backstory that birthed and enlivened the comment. What history does the speaker have with the organization? How does their personal story intersect with the institution's story? How much will the presenter stand to gain or lose with the success or failure of this proposal?

Words matter. Words represent ideas that are important and messages that are significant. Meaningful conversations must be taken at face value, but perceptive board members will also strive to understand what is taking place below the surface, and what motivated the comments.

I was invited to sit in on a board meeting for a nonprofit I admired. I was thrilled to look behind the curtain and see how they conducted their business. The meeting sailed along without much drama until its final moments. That is when a long-standing board member, an attorney by training and practice, voted *no* on a rather innocuous motion. The rest of the board looked puzzled since every other vote had been unanimous. When questioned about his *no* vote he replied, "If anyone ever reads these minutes, I want them to know that someone was awake."

His *no* vote was a one-word statement of concern over the governance practices of the board. Far more significant than his opposition to the simple motion was his challenge to the board to dig deeper, push harder, and to question more. He was saying, "We are not doing our job if we superficially rubber-stamp every proposal that comes before us."

Unfortunately, I later learned that the board member's concerns regarding the CEO were justified. His legal training, instincts, personal experience, and the prompting of the Holy Spirit, pushed him to listen attentively, probe thoughtfully, and question issues below the surface. His sensitive listening detected flaws the other board members overlooked.

Prayerful boards listen carefully and seek to understand on deeper levels.

Help me listen to the painful heart from which flows harsh comments.

The old saying reminds us, *hurt people hurt people*. The vast majority of board members have very good intentions. Their motives are pure, they want to do what is best for the organization and serve the community well. Unfortunately, not *every* board member seeks the best for all.

My consulting colleague and I presented several recommendations we thought would improve the effectiveness of a camp ministry in Middle America. One of our ideas was to relocate the maintenance building away from the front gate to the rear of the property. Consequently, the dilapidated old shed that had guarded the entrance to the camp for generations would be demolished. No longer would broken washing machines, leaky canoes, piles of lumber, and ancient lawnmowers greet campers and guests. With a few simple changes, the first impression of the camp would become a beautiful, graceful, and inviting new entranceway.

Before we finished our report, a booming voice in the back of the room shouted, "Over my dead body." I bowed up a little and was ready to push back. But before I could cause harm, my wise partner responded with a simple, yet direct question, "What are your concerns?" The disgruntled board member stepped forward and proclaimed, "That's the building where I gave my heart to Jesus 48 years ago, and it is never coming down." Like the other board members, he loved the camp. He powerfully and passionately desired to protect the ministry that God had used to transform his life. We saw the building as an eyesore. He saw it as a reminder of God's transforming grace in his life.

The conversation could have gone sideways, and it did for a while. We needed to listen to his concerns, and he needed to listen to our recommendations. Listening to each other and talking through the bigger picture allowed a new consensus to emerge.

That dialogue led to a better plan. Rather than demolition, they renovated, landscaped, and converted the old shed into a fresh, new, inviting museum, honoring the heritage of the camp. A new maintenance and storage facility, on the back of the property, became home for the more functional unsightly aspects of camp. A win-lose contest gave way to a win-win solution.

Honest, constructive dialogue led to a solution that honored the past, improved the camp's entrance experience, and helped a new generation enjoy their version of transformational camp moments. Listening to a concerned heart and responding with grace and creativity led to a God-honoring solution for all.

PRAYERFUL BOARDS

Prayerful boards seek grace-filled, and mutually beneficial solutions.

Help me learn from what is legitimate and discard what is said in spite.

Howard Hendricks, one of my favorite seminary professors, often said, "Experience is not the best teacher, evaluated experience is." We live through good times and tough times, and we should learn from both. But we often sail through the good times, enjoying the moment, doing little reflecting and self-assessment. However, we do much more soul searching when things turn sour. Sometimes criticism is unfounded, but generally, honest pushback from a concerned stakeholder is worth considering. There are often vital lessons to be learned from those tense, combative moments. We only learn from experience when we set aside our defensiveness, think about what is being said, and objectively examine our attitudes and actions in the light of God's Word.

My first boss often reminded me, "The price of leadership is to be misunderstood." Leaders are not at liberty to explain every decision they make. They often know details they cannot honorably divulge. Most people perceive issues through their limited personal lens and expect board members to see things from their vantage points as well. Board members and ministry leaders, however, live with the confounding dynamic tension of competing demands. That means some people will inevitably be disappointed, and some may become angry. Love them anyway. Board members should work to develop thick skin and a tender heart.

God called Moses to lead the whole nation out of bondage – even the troublemakers. He had followed God and done his best, but not everyone liked the changes. Some wanted to return to the good old days in Egypt. No matter the slavery, they wanted their customary foods and familiar lifestyle. Even though they were free, well cared for, heading for a new and better life, some wanted to go back to the way things used to be. *Ever heard that before?*

Fortunately for Moses, but unfortunately for his tormentors, he did not have to respond to their complaints. He merely obeyed God and stayed close to Him. The Lord opened the ground and swallowed the rebels (Numbers 16:1-35). God does not often deal with troublemakers quite so dramatically – and that is good for all of us!

It is not the job of a board to coax God onto its side of any issue or project. Rather, the job of a board is to ensure that the church or ministry is on God's side. That generally begins by demonstrating magnanimous attitudes rather than fighting for superiority or striving to win at any cost. The primary job of any church or nonprofit ministry leader is to stay close to God while loving the people he brings into their lives. That being done, leaders can have the peace, strength, courage, and wisdom needed not to overreact to harsh words or undue criticism.

Let God deal with the troublemakers in his own way. The writer of Hebrews reminds us, *For we know him who said, "It is mine to avenge; I will repay," and again, "The Lord will judge his people"* (Hebrews 10:30).

Criticism comes with the leadership territory. Along the way board members should listen well, learn all they can, develop tough hides, and maintain tender hearts.

Prayerful boards learn from honest criticism
and deflect unwarranted attacks.

Help me respond to questions with grace and respect.

Our jam-packed Chevrolet station wagon rolled slowly down an unfamiliar narrow lane in a small village on the Oregon coast. My parents looked intently at each house looking for the address we were searching for. One house looked promising but had no street numbers. My sister, brothers, and I joined the search hoping for the right address. None of us noticed the angry man unable to pass our slow-moving vehicle. Eventually his horn blared and we pulled off the road. He stopped and yelled some rude comments at my father. My eight-year-old mind said, *My dad is tougher than that guy.* But instead of fisticuffs my dad apologized. He said he was sorry and explained our situation. The angry driver mellowed, asked about the address and directed us to the house. Later my dad told us that Proverbs 15:1 was the first thought that crossed his mind, *A gentle answer turns away wrath, but a harsh word stirs up anger.*

Board meetings can become contentious, frustrating, and divisive. But how we respond to angry words and critical questions will set the tone of the meeting and dictate the atmosphere of the conversation.

Staff members spend months studying an issue, weeks preparing a report, and in the perfect world, the pertinent material is sent to the board two weeks prior to the meeting. The meeting plan calls for healthy discussion and productive dialogue. Once the deliberation starts it becomes evident that some members have not studied, let alone read, the information. Others are unaware of the key issues under review. And some are unappreciative of the work, thought, and time invested. The lack of preparation leads to indecision or tepid support.

What to do?

I tend to get exasperated and make snarky comments. "As you probably noticed on page 37..." Or "That's what I thought, until I did some research." My father gave me a better example. He helped me memorize Proverbs 15:1.

And I watched him apply this verse on multiple occasions. Board members and senior leaders of churches and non-profits should memorize this verse and practice it often.

A simple, "That's a legitimate question," or "I'm glad you asked," or "I thought someone might ask that," are sufficient to diffuse the situation and help the entire group make progress toward the desired destination.

Prayerful boards use words to build up, not tear down.

Allow me to focus on what is being said more than how I will respond.

Once I get to the gist of a comment or presume I know where a conversation is going, I tend to disengage and begin to craft my pithy, powerful, and insightful response. Most often, my end game is to win. When winning the point becomes the *primary objective*, it becomes the *exclusive objective*. And winning at *all costs* is never a healthy attitude. When we turn off the audio we fail to learn, we miss the opportunity for a deeper understanding of a new, complementary, or contradictory idea, and often, we miss the best way forward for the organization.

At least three questions will help board members listen well:

- Do I fully understand the message?
- What part(s) do I agree with and what do I find troubling?
- What size problem(s) will occur if I object and what will happen if I say nothing?

The *first* question forces us to grapple with the content. *Do I fully understand the message?* Yes, we have already established the importance of reliable data for boards to make good decisions. And we have looked at the various levels of listening to perceive content, intensity, and background. The more board members clearly understand the comments of others, the more effectively they will engage the issue. And a keen awareness of the topic under discussion is critical before moving on to the next two questions.

The *second* question forces board members to analyze the content of the issue being deliberated and to make healthy value judgments. *What part(s) do I agree with and what do I find troubling?* Not all ideas are worthwhile, and not all proposals align well with the church or nonprofit's stated goals, shared values, or cultural realities. Board members must set aside personal friendships and be willing to risk rejection as they filter plans and assess what they think is best for the institution.

Listening need not always be about accepting or rejecting. More importantly, listening should involve gaining understanding and searching for common ground. Points of agreement become critical building blocks to form coalitions and to create an atmosphere of support and affirmation. Identifying and highlighting widely affirmed topics provides a significant backdrop of unity. A harmonious starting point creates a context of grace, and grace provides room for constructive interaction when conflicting ideas arise. Affirming two or three key points of any proposal sets the stage for a more collegial discussion on topics of disagreement.

The *third* question deals with the cost-benefit issue. "What size problem(s) may occur if I object, and what will result if I say nothing?" This question really asks, "Is this worth a fight?" Board members must ask themselves, "Is this a big deal, or will my contradictory comments make it a big deal?" Undeniably, there are moral and ethical commitments, corporate beliefs, missional responsibilities, and core values that need to be protected, but most fights occur over preferred methodology, desired practices, and who will hold the power. "So, what if the issue goes against my personal preferences? Will the institution suffer significant damage if I don't get my way?" Board members don't have to prove they are the smartest person in the room on every issue. They must always evaluate the topics under consideration in relation to the big picture. "What are the upside opportunities and downside risks? What damage could happen to the institution if I do not object? What damage could happen to my relationships within the board if I object? Is this a mountain I want to die upon?" Picking battles wisely is a critical skill of all good board members.

Prayerful boards listen carefully and respond cautiously.

Personal Reflections

Are you a good listener? What can you do to become better at this essential skill?

Can you recall a painful board discussion that could have been avoided by better listening skills?

What is your normal response when your ideas face objections or outright rejection? Is there a better possible response?

Can you recall a time during a board discussion when a gentle answer turned away anger?

Board Discussion

What are some questions the board could review before each meeting to set the tone for good listening?

Have there been times when this board has been criticized unjustly? How did the board respond and was that a God-honoring response?

Grade the overall listening ability of the board on a scale of A+ to F-.

What can this board do to encourage better listening and gentler responses?

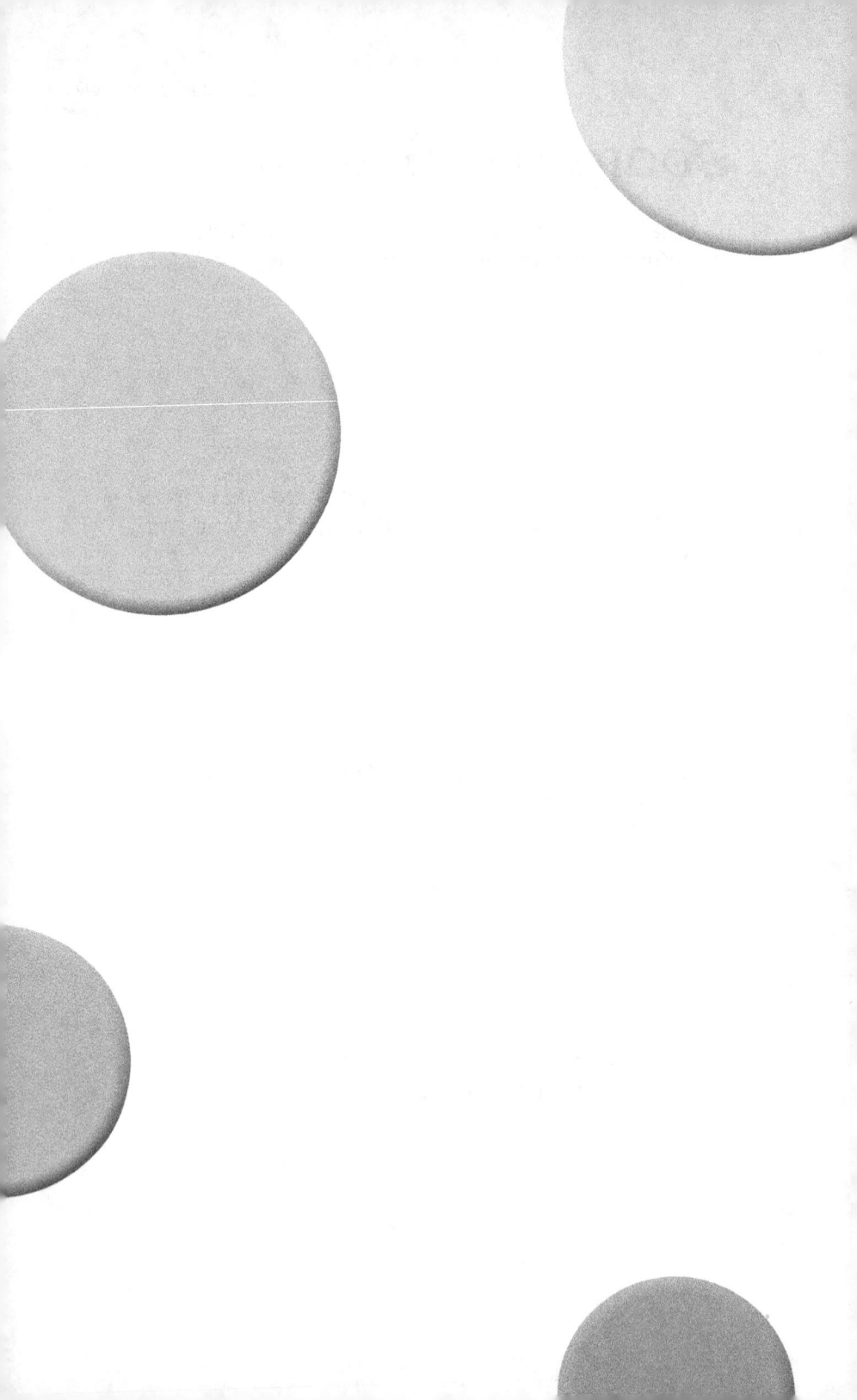

CHAPTER 5

SPEAK CAUTIOUSLY

Help me speak cautiously.

I enjoy a great fire! Whether an engaging fireplace, marsh-mallow roast, campfire, or bonfire, I am drawn to the flames. At times I have been accused of being a little cav-alier with the flames. Over the years, the local volunteer fire department knew the way to our property all too well. Their first visit was a few days after I burned a big pile of leaves. In my defense, the fire looked like it was out. And we really didn't need the small shed at the end of our driveway!

Fire, like conversations, can be delightful or destructive. A significant part of what boards do is talk. In committees, in sidebar conversations, and to the watching stakeholders, boards use words, and words matter. James warns us that speech is a two-edged sword, tremendously beneficial but at times potentially destructive. To illustrate his point, James uses the potent and intriguing image of fire. He says,

> *How great a forest is set ablaze by such a small fire! And the tongue is a fire, . . . With it we bless our Lord and Father, and with it we curse people who are made in the likeness of God. From the same mouth come blessing and cursing.* (James 3:5b-10a ESV)

Fire, that wonderful gift that cooks our food, heats our water, warms our houses, and creates cheery fireplace environments, can also be very destructive. This amazing element that roasts marshmallows, creates a romantic candlelight dinner, and brings great delight to us all, can also inflict excruciating pain, destroy what it touches, turn homes into rubble, and scorch everything in its path. So too, our words.

The problem is much larger than the boardroom. Poorly spoken words can damage any relationship. Fortunately, words can also do immense good. They encourage, instruct, warn, inspire, and express our deepest thoughts and heartfelt emotions. Aptly spoken words are the best of the best. They are extremely valuable, *Like apples of gold in settings of silver* (Proverbs 25:11).

The word *aptly* is derived from the Greek root that means *suitable* or *fit*. This same root gives us words like appropriate and aptitude. The general idea is that aptly spoken words are *suitable* words that *fit* the occasion. At times words that are strong and forceful are aptly spoken. Other situations call for aptly spoken words that are calm and soothing.

We should use words with great caution. The same hammer that builds up can also tear down. The delights and benefits of fire can quickly pivot and become hurtful and destructive. We must choose our words well and use them wisely. That is true in all of life, but the benefits and threats of our words are magnified in the boardroom.

Prayerful boards understand the power of words and use them cautiously.

L et me use the fewest words, the least intensity, and the lowest volume needed to be understood.

People serving on boards or working for boards use words to offer their opinions, shape thoughts, re-craft concepts, articulate goals, and create consensus. Board members *should* express their ideas, share their thoughts, provide input, and participate in the discussion. Contributing their perspectives and wisdom makes their service valuable. But at times, the warmth of some board members' comments can burn hot, too hot. Their words run away with them and generate more heat than light.

Verbal intensity and increased volume are not bad things. Ideas need to be articulated and expressed with enthusiasm and passion. At times, the volume must be raised to emphasize an idea. But for every action there is a reaction. Each time we strive to make a point by speaking more rapidly, heightening the pitch, and increasing the volume, we draw a line in the sand. Those who support the idea are more inclined to defend it, but those with an opposing position now reject the proposal both on its merit and style points. Some board members might be swayed to support an issue by the intensity of the presentation, but the bravado may turn away other members sitting on the fence.

Winning and losing are part of every board's reality, but too much intensity and volume puts competition center stage. A much better approach is to listen more, ratchet back the intensity and volume, and strive to find common ground. The goal is to develop a level of emotional engagement that generates excitement, encourages discussion, clarifies ideas, and creates outcomes that are better than any individual could produce on his or her own.

Ongoing presentations, with high pitched and rapidly spoken arguments, along with loud pulpit pounding bravado may stroke egos and intimidate weak board members. However, those who make a pattern of such behavior tend to demonstrate their need to be right more than their desire to find God's path forward. Yes, we need to hold strongly to many of our positions. And we need to be able to sell our ideas if we believe they represent the best path forward. However, the plans we support should stand on the cut of the steak, not the seduction of the sizzle.

People listen more when we speak less. Stay calm and turn down the volume.

Prayerful boards strive for understanding, not victory.

Help me voice my opinions with care, strength, and meekness.

Board members carry a responsibility to voice their opinions. They are expected to contribute their wisdom and perspectives to the corporate decision-making process. But *how* that is done is at least as important as *what* is expressed. To bite one's tongue and say nothing robs the group of a valuable perspective, the board needs to hear all perspectives. But expressing opinions with care is critical. Saying nothing is not a good solution, but neither are rude, angry, or combative statements. The middle ground, where board members contribute gracious, thoughtful, and articulate comments and ask pertinent, clarifying questions, should be the goal. Robust opinions are essential, but they should be stated with care, strength, and meekness.

Share opinions with care. It is always a good idea to think before speaking, but at times, as board discussions banter back and forth, there is little time to polish thoughts – words tumble out. Disclaimers, at the beginning or the end of a statement, can help soften the impact of reckless words. "I haven't thought this through as much as I'd like but it seems to me . . . ." *Or*, "I might be wrong, but my gut tells me . . . . What do the rest of you think?" *Or*, "I'm not sure if this is the best answer, but I'll toss it out and get your reaction. It seems to me that . . . ." Inviting pushback is also a graceful way to proceed. "Here is my idea but I know that together we can make it better." *Or*, "My preference would be . . . . Help me see what's wrong with this idea."

Express opinions with strength. Board members need not be wishy-washy about their opinions. They should be unafraid to encourage others to support valid proposals. But they need to compel others to join their position based upon the strength of the argument, not the volume of the presentation. Adequate and accurate information, clear presentations, ideas tied to the mission, and concepts that flow toward defined objectives provide the strength needed to express opinions effectively.

Share opinions with meekness. The world tends to equate *meekness* with *weakness*. People who are meek are thought to be compliant, non-assertive, and easily swayed. From a Christian perspective, nothing could be farther from the truth. The biblical picture of meekness is *power under control*. As a horse applies its strength to the wishes of its rider, it does not become weak – merely effective. Meekness for board members means that they express their opinions, not to win a debate, but to help the group find the best solution, answer, or plan. Meekness allows powerful board members to present their views, not as win-lose propositions, but as significant contributions to the group's discernment of the best path forward.

How we begin has a huge influence on how we end. And that is certainly true of board meetings. Starting each meeting with prayer for guidance and a reminder of the ground rules helps set the stage for the discussion to fol-low. Reminding the board members of three basic meeting rules may be helpful:

- Express your thoughts to the group. Each member's perspective is significant and valuable.
- Share your thoughts concisely – don't monopolize the discussion.
- Don't present final drafts, present proposals. Every idea can be improved.

Managing a meeting and reminding board members to voice opinions with care, strength, and meekness falls on the shoulders of the board chair. The skill and demeanor of the board chair can make or break a meeting. Wise board chairs *encourage* discussion, *control* discussion, and *refine* discussion.

Prayerful boards express opinions with care, strength, and meekness.

Help me ask good questions, open dialogue, explore options, and deepen discussion.

There are two ways to play ping-pong. The *first* is to serve hard and fast, working for a shot that cannot be returned. Slam the return or smother it with topspin, anything so your opponent's return finds the net or flies off the end of the table. Back and forth, trying to end the rally with the next furious blast. The goal is to win the point and defeat the opponent. The *second* method is to work together to see how long you can extend the rally. Back and forth, back and forth, easy lobs, few mistakes, ongoing repetition, forever and forever, always trying to avoid making a mistake and striving to continue the gentle process to avoid a conclusion. In ping-pong and in board meetings, danger lurks at both extremes. Healthy boards navigate a middle pathway.

Some board members play to win. They strive to make their point and deliver the kill-shot early, shutting down the competition and the conversation. They blast away and then position themselves to meet the challenge of an aggressive return.

During one of my first board meetings as a young CEO, two board members squared off. I presented a plan that required borrowing a relatively small amount of money and waited for what I assumed would be a few supportive comments and quick, unanimous approval. That proved to be a very poor assumption. The first comment came from a godly, strong, and fiscally conservative financial expert. He forcefully said, "God does not bless ministries that borrow money." The room became quiet before an equally godly, powerful, experienced risk-taker shot back, "Time is running out. Jesus is coming back and when he does, I want to go out borrowed up – let the Devil pay the mortgage!" Game on!

After a brief rally of smash and return smash, kill shot and return kill shot, cooler heads prevailed. The rally began. Back and forth, back and forth, the broader discussion continued for an agonizingly long time. Eventually, they made a decision and established a policy regarding when the ministry could borrow money.

Kill shots rarely lead to good board decisions. Rallies that engage multiple board members who concisely share their insights and expertise generally lead to healthier board deliberations. However, rallies can go on and on ad nauseam. A happy medium should be found that opens discussion and stays focused. The challenge is to find the healthy space between overpowering, domineering free-for-alls, and pointless conversations that flow on and on.

To help deepen discussion and open new perspectives on critical subjects consider using:

- Consultants
- Break-out groups
- *What-if* scenarios
- Personal position statements
- Surveys
- One-word reports
- Straw votes

A board should not make a decision until each member is comfortable that his or her opinion has been aired thoroughly. Stampeding a decision through the process may seem efficient, but if board members feel coerced, steamrolled, ignored, or manipulated, they will never be fully supportive. However, board members whose ideas have contributed to a better, more comprehensive outcome are the ones most likely to implement the plan. One of my mentors often reminded me, "People like to play in treehouses they help build."

PRAYERFUL BOARDS

Prayerful boards realize that healthy deliberation leads to healthy outcomes.

Help me say nothing degrading and nothing that would draw lines of conflict unnecessarily.

I placed a major proposal on the table. The outcome would reshape the ministry for years to come. Money, energy, priorities, and institutional direction were on the line. There were many facts, but more unknowns. The potential for growth and expanded ministry was enormous, but the risks were also high. Strong opinions were expressed on both sides of the issue. Several sat on the fence listening, learning, wrestling with the alternatives, and praying for divine guidance.

Three questions rolled over and over as I prepared for the meeting. *First*, "What if my proposal is defeated?" The hopes and dreams of many of us would be crushed, and my leadership credibility would rightly be called into question. How would I feel toward those who rejected my plan? *Second*, "What if the motion passes? What would happen to the board members who argued against the proposal? Would they feel ostracized and diminished?" And of course, my *third* terrifying question was, "If the proposal passes, how will we ever see it through to reality?"

A wise consultant who helped us through the planning process and who sensed the tension in earlier meetings arrived with his reports and plans, but also with a box of Breathe Right® nasal strips. Before the discussion everyone in the room, board members, staff members, and consultants, put a Breathe-Right® strip on their nose. These small, white strips are designed to help the wearer breathe more comfortably. They allow the air to move unhindered through the nasal passages and into one's body. We all needed to breathe right that day. We needed the Holy Spirit to guide us toward the best outcome, but we also needed Him to help us deliberate in a God-honoring way. We prayed for God's will to be done, and we prayed that we would become more unified through a noble, civil, and collaborative process.

The robust discussion was remarkably gracious. The white strips across our noses provided a visual reminder that the *process* was as critical as the *outcome*. Everyone wanted the same result; the discussion was always about the best path forward. Questions were in the form of legitimate concerns that focused on issues, not people. The chairman even-handedly allowed the rally to proceed while keeping the discussion on point. By honoring all opinions and prayerfully striving to discern God's will, not win the point, the board was able to move forward with unity. The discussion remained focused on the issue and never became personal. We modified the plans to address legitimate concerns. The decision was close, one vote decided the issue.

In the end, all the board members supported the outcome because they believed in the process and were committed to honoring God throughout the deliberations. Those who voted against the plan became supportive and endorsed the new path forward. The Breathe-Right® strips reminded us of the two-part goal. First, discover God's heart for the future of the ministry. And second, proceed in a way that reflects God's presence throughout the process.

Prayerful boards address challenging issues in God-honoring ways.

H elp me affirm and agree whenever possible.

South Dakota term limits required my older brother Jim to leave the state legislature after 16 years. He served eight years in the House and eight years in the Senate. To honor him, my younger brother, Paul, and I went to Pierre for the last few days of his final legislative session. Many people complimented him and told us stories about his contribution to the legislative process.

South Dakota is basically a one-party state. When he left, 30 of the 35 senators were Republicans. As we walked out the door for the final exit, a tall, stately senator hurried to meet us. He was a Democrat and represented his predominantly native-American district. He told us that he arrived in the Senate with a great deal of skepticism. He expected continual fighting and little support. He then shared a story about his first legislative initiative to provide greater educational funding for children on the reservations. He said the first person to speak was my brother Jim, who argued in favor of the legislation, supporting the motion for providing the best education possible for every child in the State.

The senator went on to tell us that those comments won the day. The legislation passed, his hope was rekindled, and he realized that there were opportunities to work together.

Why not look for points of unity? Why not look for common ground?

Ben Sasse, in his book, *Them: Why We Hate Each Other -- and How to Heal*, says, "When we start from the assumption that our opponents are like us---decent folks who want what's best but who start from a different place---we are more likely to be respectful and to have a conversation that is productive" (page 163-164). Earlier he commented on how neighbors can live with differences yet enjoy respectful harmony. He said, "Neighbors see today's conversation not as the last conversation we will ever have, but as a precursor to tomorrow's" (page 162).

Switzerland has been a neutral country since 1815. Since the days of Napoleon, the Swiss have avoided armed conflict with their neighbors. When the board faces potentially divisive issues, look for your church or ministry's Switzerland. Where is the *neutral ground* of agreement? Where can discussion begin? What are the common commitments that we affirm? What shared factors can provide bridges over which constructive dialogue can travel?

Three places to look for neutral ground, that may help avoid potentially divisive conversations are the *past, present*, and *future*. Board members may find unifying starting points with comments such as:

The Past
- This ministry has been though some tough times, and we have seen God work in remarkable ways.
- Seven years ago, we didn't know if we would make it through the end of the fiscal year. And here we are.
- By God's grace, since this ministry started, 10,000 peoples' lives have been changed.

The Present
- We are experiencing an amazing constellation of strong staff, growing programs, and financial support.
- This is the first time that our board has faced this type of challenge. We can get through this together.
- God has brought the right people to the board table for such a time as this.

The Future
- I know that we all want to see this ministry grow and thrive for years to come.
- We wouldn't be here tonight if we didn't believe that God has significant opportunities for this church in the days ahead.
- Twenty years from now, our children, and thousands more, will benefit from what we decide tonight.

Find your *Switzerland.* Use that point of unity to build trust and camaraderie. Remember, most of the time, everyone wants the best outcome for the most people. Differences regarding methodology need not degenerate into win-lose contests. Look for common ground and use that building site to construct the best outcomes possible.

Prayerful boards discover neutral ground to establish plans and build unity.

Help me give second-voice to a courageous and wise first-voice; those who risk presenting a new, contrary, or unrefined perspective.

Many good ideas arise in humble fashion. They are messy and unrefined, and at times they present a new or contrarian perspective. A new idea needs a champion to present the concept. But they also need someone to come alongside and provide support.

An argument can be made that the *first follower* is the *true leader.* Unless there is a willing follower, there is not a functional leader. As the old saying goes, "If you think you are leading but no one is following, you are just taking a walk!" Until a person has at least one follower, they are not truly leading. The first follower validates the initial leader and becomes the gatekeeper for additional support. Once the first follower steps forward, the door opens for others to join the cause.

Once new ideas are expressed, they will go one of three directions:

- Some will hang in the air and die an agonizing death as the trial balloon slowly deflates to the thunderous sound of awkward silence.
- Others are eagerly embraced. They resonate with the opinion of leaders in the room and gain immediate support.
- However, many proposals hang in the balance, tottering between acceptance and extinction. The awkward suspension ends when a bravehearted colleague supports the concept, often asking for clarification, greater refinement, or additional study.

The writer of Ecclesiastes observes that *Two are better than one* (Ecclesiastes 4:9). But when it comes to new and risky ideas, two are *way* better than one. *They have a good return for their work.* The person who generates the novel idea does his or her part by putting the proposal into play. But the first person to speak, to support or denounce the concept, performs a critical role as well. Either they give strength and credibility to the new idea, opening the door for others to lend their support, or they throw cold water on the idea, extinguishing the creative flame.

Prayerful boards look for the creative kernel within every new idea.

Lord, help me accept compliments and approval with humility.

Church and nonprofit boards, just like their individual members, have good days and bad days, ups and downs, wins and losses. During tough days, compliments provide energy for the journey. I kept a "happy file" in my desk drawer filled with thank-you notes, letters of appreciation, and supportive memorabilia. When I had one of those days when all four wheels came off, I would open the file and remember better days. Encouraging comments mute, but do not silence, harsh words of criticism.

When those we value, respect, and admire, approve of our work and appreciate our accomplishments, we tend to enthusiastically respond with increased effort and greater creativity. As the adage goes, "Nothing succeeds like success." We need to hear positive comments that keep us encouraged and focused.

My friend worked for a godly, but somewhat detached supervisor. When he suggested that his boss might want to offer a special word of encouragement to an employee who had experienced a major milestone and served their ministry well, the boss responded, "Why? That's why I pay him!" Yes, staff, paid and unpaid, do not work for human praise, but expressions of appreciation mean a great deal. Management studies consistently show that appreciation for a job well done is a powerful motivator.

More importantly than the pragmatic benefits of a well-earned *attaboy*, God commands encouragement. A significant New Testament directive is to *encourage one another* (1 Thessalonians 4:18 and 5:11). Encouragement is not a nice "add-on" to our personal and professional relationships, it is essential. We need to give and receive words of affirmation. We need to hear when we are doing well, and we need to pass along compliments to those who work alongside us.

Compliments and approval can, however, be treacherous. They prey on the vulnerable dark side of our souls. The praise of people can become the adrenaline that feeds our egos and creates the rush that motivates us toward an imbalanced life and self-aggrandized perception of our significance to the institution. Human approval becomes the cheese we seek at the end of our ministry maze. The rewards of this world are a poor substitute for God's commendation, *Well done, good and faithful servant.*

Accepting affirming words cautiously is always a good idea. Three considerations may help us remain balanced when compliments come our way.

Is this praise legitimate? Sometimes kind and encouraging words are merely flattery. Inauthentic supportive comments may attempt to create an on-ramp for an undeserved favor. We want to believe the half-truths and comments that shade reality in our favor. Humility allows us to filter authentic comments of support from self-serving flattery.

Are there others who should share this moment of honor? We rarely achieve significant accomplishments without a team of contributors. Humility guides us to share the spotlight with others and expand the ring of honor. Oddly, sharing praise in moments of success does not diminish well-deserved recognition. Rather the award is multiplied and grows throughout the organization.

Is God glorified? John the Baptist was creating quite a stir. People were coming to him, confessing their sins, and being baptized as an act of repentance. The Jewish religious leaders interrogated John asking *Who are you?* John first responded in the negative. *I am not the Christ* (John 1:20), and second, he said, *I am the voice of one calling in the desert, make straight the way of the Lord* (John 1:23). Humbly glorifying God means that we do not claim to be who we are not. God alone provides us the capacities to do what we do. Second, we clearly understand what God calls us to do and affirm the role that he allows us to play.

PRAYERFUL BOARDS

Prayerful boards give and receive meaningful compliments.

G ive me the grace to watch with dignity as my proposal fails and give me humility when my idea meets with approval.

When things go well, we should praise God, share the credit with others, and humbly thank the one who has noticed and affirmed the success. But things don't always go well. Not every project succeeds, and not every idea is met with cheers and rounds of applause.

We must embrace one of two fundamental responses when the board rejects our plans, selects a pathway contrary to our wishes, or makes a seemingly poor choice (assuming that the decision is not immoral or unethical.) One, we can pout – openly or internally. Outwardly brash, harsh, or punitive statements rarely accomplish much. And inwardly, the bitter attitudes of our hearts gnaw at our souls. Outward or inward resentment certainly widens the relational divide that we must overcome before the next divisive issue arises.

Or two, we can trust God, become a team player, and support the prescribed action. We can accept the reality that God is working on a bigger plan than we can imagine and that he is in control.

We cannot completely forget our failures, hurts, and rejections, but we can consciously commit to disregard those painful memories to the best of our ability. To do that, our challenge is twofold. First, avoid the urge to say, "I told you so." And second, empty the suitcase of past pain, allowing us to objectively address each ensuing issue with fresh perspective and unbiased enthusiasm.

The writer of Hebrews explains the process of getting past our grievances and seeing the bigger picture:

Make every effort to live in peace with all men and to be holy; without holiness no one will see the Lord. See to it that no one misses the grace of God and that no bitter root grows up to cause trouble and defile many. (Hebrews 12:14-15)

These verses have four simple directives that will help us avoid bitterness and move past our painful defeats.

Make every effort to live in peace. Ministry leaders should work to maintain peaceful relationships and strive to get along with each other as best they can. They should avoid making hurtful comments, search for common ground, and give others the benefit of the doubt whenever possible.

Be holy. No one is perfect, but board members should strive to live holy lives. Personally and corporately board members should live in ways that please God and honor him. Sexual transgression and financial misconduct are two significant danger zones. Missteps in either of these arenas bring down ministries and individuals with devastating and long-term consequences. Board members personify the organizations they represent. For better or worse, board members are often seen as the embodiment of their institutions. Their personal sins leave indelible marks on the churches and nonprofits they represent.

See to it that no one misses the grace of God. Focus on God's grace. When leaders are forced into a hard decision, they should consider erring on the side of grace, remembering all that God has done for them and for the institution they represent. Churches and nonprofits and their leaders must not forget that it is God's ministry and that he graciously allows them the joy of serving with him. Pause and take time to thank God for the gifts that come from his hand and extend grace to those around the board table.

See to it that . . . no bitter root grows up to cause trouble and defile many. Bitterness finds it difficult to take root in the soil of peace, holiness, grace, and forgiveness. Boards filled with these godly qualities leave little room for bitterness to grow.

PRAYERFUL BOARDS

Prayerful boards are humble and gracious;
they afford bitterness no room to grow.

Personal Reflections

○ When you want to make a point, do you tend to increase your volume, speed up your speech, raise your pitch, or employ some other method of intensity?

○ How have you demonstrated meekness in board meetings? What was the result?

○ Do you tend to attack, engage in healthy dialogue, or withdraw from contrary and conflicting opinions?

○ Have you made every effort to live in peace with the other board members? If not, what can you do to encourage a better, healthier relationship?

Board Discussion

● *What are some preparatory statements that board members could use to soften the resistance to new, unrefined, or contrarian opinions?*

● *What are some healthy methods the board could employ to deepen discussion and surface additional perspectives?*

● *Is there an issue on the board's agenda or on the horizon that might require a stop at the store for Breathe Right© strips?*

● *What recent success or accomplishment by a staff member or volunteer should be noted and honored by the board?*

CHAPTER 6

PLAN WISELY

Dear God, give the board wisdom to plan wisely.

King David envisioned a great temple to honor and worship God. The Ark of the Covenant had remained in the Tabernacle, being borderline homeless, long enough. David wanted to build a grand and permanent home for the Ark where the nation could gather for praise, fellowship, and worship. He shared his plan with his trusted and godly advisor, Nathan the prophet. Nathan had delivered bad news to David in the past, now he could happily support this powerful and pious new undertaking. The Chronicler shares the story:

After David was settled in his palace, he said to Nathan the prophet, "Here I am, living in a palace of cedar, while the ark of the covenant of the LORD is under a tent." Nathan replied to David, "Whatever you have in mind, do it, for God is with you." (1 Chronicles 17:1-2)

David's planning process followed the well-practiced pattern many leaders employ today. One person has an idea, they share their dream with a few trusted friends, encouraging conversations ensue and things begin to steam-roll. Despite David's good intentions, God had a better idea. God shared his design with Nathan, and plans quickly went in a different direction. *That night the word of God came to Nathan, saying: "Go and tell my servant David, 'This is what the LORD says: You are not the one to build me a house to dwell in'"* (1 Chronicles 17:3-4).

One of a board's most challenging responsibilities is to discover God's design for the future of the church or ministry. Some board decisions are rather mundane, routine, and have minimal long-term impact. However, strategic planning decisions require boards to use great discernment and to consider long-term implications. Board planning peers intently along the farthest and widest horizon. Board decisions often impact the greatest number of people for the longest amount of time.

It may appear to be a mere semantic difference, however, as I mentioned in chapter three, the work of the board is not vision *casting*, rather vision *discovery*. For Christian churches and ministries, the process is not thinking up the next best idea. A board's challenge is always one of *discerning* God's will and *discovering* his direction.

Board decisions impact everyone within the organization, and they have the longest shelf-life of all decisions made by the institution. Planning should be done prayerfully and with a desire to discern God's prescribed pathway for the institution. David's idea was good, but he wasn't God's choice to see it through to completion. Great and godly leaders play their parts, they contribute their gifts and abilities to the process, but they remember, the plan is God's. Their role is to discern God's will and fulfill it faithfully.

Prayerful boards seek to discern God's plan for their institution's future.

Help us see opportunities and threats and count the cost as we weigh risks and rewards.

Planning can be tedious and challenging, but in some ways, it is quite simple and direct. Consider sailing. Every sailor planning a trip asks two important questions. *First*, before climbing aboard and setting sail, they ask, *what is the condition of the ship*? Sailors check the hull, rudder, sails, lines, provisions, communication equipment, life preservers, and a host of other elements. Church and non-profit boards should follow the same pattern. They must learn all they can about the condition of their institutional ship: staff, finances, programs, communication, facilities, equipment, marketing, technology, and of course, the board itself.

Second, sailors check the weather report. The crew can *discover* and *resolve* problems they find within the ship when they ask the first question. However, they can only *observe and respond* to the weather conditions around them. So too, boards possess the ability to correct deficiencies within their institution, but they must also read the weather report and respond wisely as conditions change around them. Uncontrollable external considerations for boards to review include economic realities, demographic shifts, social changes, cultural norms, legal requirements, and environmental factors.

Assess each external threat and opportunity based upon the twin factors of probability and potential impact. If the weather report calls for a hurricane in the Caribbean, and a ministry resides along the coast near Galveston, Texas, the probability is high that the storm will strike the area. If landfall occurs near Galveston, the potential impact upon the ministry is high. High probability and high impact issues should lead the board to consider a change of course. However, if the same storm is brewing, and your ministry is located 500-miles north in Little Rock, the probability is low that damaging wind and rain will reach that far inland. If the storm arrives, it will probably be little more than a nuisance with minimal impact. Low probability and low impact events require little board attention.

Boards need to ask some challenging questions. What does the weather report tell us about the current chances of raising significant funds, enlisting more volunteers, launching new programs, or hiring well-qualified staff? What needs are growing? What cultural, societal, political, economic, and environmental shifts are rolling through the ministry's world?

The *internal* strengths and weaknesses of the ship must be coordinated with the *external* opportunities and threats of the weather report. God's will is often discerned as these internal and external realities are clearly identified and courageously addressed.

Prayerful boards look inside and outside the ministry with honest and discerning eyes.

H elp us see the possibilities for a better future.

Looking at the same wallpaper day after day makes it disappear – at least in our minds. The longer we live with that pattern, the more it goes unnoticed. On rare occasions, when we do take a closer look, we believe the pattern is right and proper. We assume that it should remain that way forever, we cannot imagine any other design. An occasional shake-up helps a board see the world with new clarity. Fresh eyes enable a board to move past the *same-old, same-old* perspectives. Rotating board membership is not just a way to minimize burnout or to unload ineffective or overbearing board members. It is also a way to ensure that fresh viewpoints address persistent and entrenched problems. New members bring fresh ideas, refreshing hope, and unfettered possibilities.

Consultants can also help identify opportunities that may be hiding in the tall weeds of unaddressed problems. Often a consultant's eyes have seen similar situations in different contexts. Their unique vantage point can surface possible solutions or provide guidance to a better outcome.

The best eyes may be the eyes of those served. Parishioners, listeners, students, campers, or patients will see the ministry from a different point of view than the staff or the board. Developing easy and immediate feedback opportunities can provide excellent new information to help plan and move forward.

While directing a family camp, I would often ask the guests to provide me with their suggestions on how to make the camp better next summer. I would tell them that I was not very smart or creative, but I could read! Their ideas fueled the changes needed to better serve future guests.

Every board member's job is to help the organization move toward a better future. But the desire for growth, improvement, and greater effectiveness can become treacherously seductive. Every board should ask three questions while striving to move into that brighter future.

How do we protect our present constituency? Can we continue to provide our current clients and stakeholders with the services they have come to expect while we engage a new challenge? How do we care for our elementary students while we add a high school? How do we build a residential camp while still serving our day campers? Or how do we continue to feed the hungry while establishing a drug rehabilitation center? Change can siphon money, energy, creativity, and attention away from current programs and current clients. Boards must ensure that unintentional neglect does not compromise the ongoing ministry.

Is this too much too soon? Significant organizational changes that take a church or ministry in a radically new direction can create tremendous torque on the institution. Churches and ministry organizations can implode in the face of chaotic redesign. Too much change at too rapid a pace can create an unstable environment where staff leave, systems fail, donors become bewildered, parishioners move on, and clients look elsewhere for services.

Is this enough change to generate enthusiasm? Change that merely puts new paint on old buildings is not the change that inspires the staff, draws volunteers to commit, or donors to give. New visions must engage and challenge people with hope that the sacrifices and investments they make will contribute to transformed lives, a better world, and God's glory.

There will always be those who resist innovation, no matter how beneficial. Some Israelites preferred life in Egypt, with its familiar diet and predictable routines, even though it meant a return to slavery. Some were overwhelmed and threatened by the unfamiliar food God provided and the unknown outcomes of their new adventure. They preferred caution over courage and fear over faith.

Wise leaders understand the ephemeral nature of donors' and volunteers' commitments to churches and nonprofits. They vote with their wallets and their feet. The challenge for boards is to find a healthy balance between enough change to engage and enthuse parishioners, listeners, campers, students, and clients, while not generating so much torque that damage is done to the good work that is underway.

A better future does not mean maintaining the past, destroying the present, or jeopardizing the future. Boards are called to prayerfully discern God's will, seek the best possible future, and shepherd the ministry to that better place.

Prayerful boards ask God to guide them as they embrace new opportunities.

Help us honor the past and give us the courage to abandon the methods that provided yesterday's success but will lead to futility tomorrow.

A trapeze artist must let go of one bar before sailing gracefully through open air to grasp the swing that awaits. Whether driven by courage or craziness, the artist must let go of his or her security to reach the desired destination. It is true of high-wire acts and it is true of ministries. Churches and organizations tend to cling to the programs and methodologies that provided yesterday's success and security. Too often leaders assume that the next generation needs the programs of the past and fail to see the distinction between *outcomes* and *methods*. The desired outcomes of churches and ministries should remain relatively constant year after year. Their methods, however, should stay fluid, adapting to the times to accommodate the changing realities of their ministry context.

Every church or nonprofit has desired outcomes: growing parishioners, healthy patients, educated students, sober clients, happy campers, or trained leaders. And every ministry modifies its methods – intentionally or not.

For over 2,000 years the medical world used leeches extensively to treat patients. Only a few very specialized procedures use these slimy creatures today. Hardbound encyclopedias were a staple in every classroom a generation ago, today data is available with the tap of a screen. The world changes and so must ministry methodologies if boards expect their ministries to stay viable and effective. As Peter Drucker said, "Innovate or die."

But change for the sake of change can be reckless. New programs and ideas should be vetted against the Word of God, as well as the mission, values, and desired outcomes of the ministry. Stagnant boards can easily slip into a mode where planning begins by considering available alternatives rather than desired outcomes. Boards tend to ask, "What can we do?" And the answer is generally, "What we did last year" or, "What will be easiest?" A much better approach is to start with the question, "What *should* we do?" That question returns the board to the church or nonprofit's mission, values, and desired outcomes. A key board responsibility is to ensure that the church or ministry remains focused on effectiveness, rather than the expediency of the decision making process. Questions that deal with *should* provide the sieve through which the board and leadership staff can sift the available options to determine which one will be the most effective in achieving the ministry's objectives.

The answer to the question, "What *should* we do?" may lead to the painful reality that the organization needs to say goodbye to some dearly loved and deeply appreciated programs. Wise boards take great care to honor the past and express appreciation to those who have invested much in the success of days now fading into history. But honoring the past is much better than repeating it into obsolescence – just ask the leading manufacturer of eight-track tapes 50 years ago!

Prayerful boards honor the past and yet seek current effectiveness to protect the future.

Help us discover and employ the most effective methods to accomplish your mission for this ministry in the days ahead.

Developing and implementing new programs is a perilous mission, but boards must look into the future and set the course for the years to come. Some trends play out as predicted, but others seem to be aberrations. And even when the trends are understood correctly, the ripple effects can be miscalculated.

I graduated college in 1975 and took my first ministry leadership role as a camp program director. I was invited to attend a meeting with a futurist who assessed and shared trends that would impact the Christian camping world in the coming years. His major point was that computers would soon become common place. These monstrous machines that currently filled entire floors in academic, government, and commercial buildings and were cooled by high powered air-conditioners, would soon shrink drastically. Eventually, every worker would have a computer on his or her desk. As amazing as that crystal-ball wizardry was, his next conclusion was even more stunning. Due to the available computing power, people would become more and more efficient and complete their work in much less time. Weekends would grow, vacations would extend, discretionary time would mushroom. Two-day work weeks and five-day weekends were just around the corner. The futurist challenged the Christian camping community to prepare for the onslaught of people looking for ways to sop up their increased discretionary time. He was right on the coming technological change, but wrong on the ramifications for our lives.

Boards make the best predictions possible and adapt their ministry's approach as needed. Using consultants, reading widely, attending seminars, and processing current events are all important aspects of planning. That is why boards prosper when they have many insightful perspectives contributing to the discussion. Solomon was the wisest man who ever lived, yet he surrounded himself with advisors. He was wise enough to know that even he had blind spots and needed additional perspectives to guide his decisions. He wrote, *Plans fail for lack of counsel, but with many advisers they succeed* (Proverbs 15:22).

Four simple practices may help boards stay current, adapt well to the ever-changing environment, and discern God's plan for the future.

Bathe the process in prayer. When new ideas emerge, as plans develop, and dreams take shape, ask God to open your eyes to new and more effective possibilities. Ask God to blow away the chaff of your poor decisions and to help you discover what will be most effective.

Interact with the broader community. Associations, denominations, conferences, or kindred groups allow churches, schools, hospitals, camps, radio stations, mission agencies, or any other sector of the ministry community to cross-pollinate. Other boards that lead similar organizations face parallel challenges and deal with related problems. Dialogue over mutual concerns can generate valuable synergy. We learn much from one another. There is strength in numbers.

Take a field trip. Boards can learn a great deal by visiting similar ministries that are bigger, older, or more effective. Meeting with others working in the same geographic neighborhood can build camaraderie and foster healthy discussions concerning common concerns. Friendly competition between ministries working in close proximity may limit the free-flow of ideas. Distance creates freedom that allows deeper and more collegial discussions. Interacting with those a little farther down the road enlightens board members and expands their horizons for greater vision.

Tap into the board's network of experienced associates. Each board member has friends and co-workers who have expertise in areas where the organization struggles. Board members can facilitate a richer discussion and build a better future by enlisting the professional expertise of their friends. The volunteers they bring into the organization add value and strength to the planning discussions. An architect may provide questions to ask the design firm bidding on the next big project. A land developer may add perspective on expansion decisions. A computer expert may do an audit of the ministry's IT systems. Or a teacher may evaluate the organization's instructional materials. Board members help shape the future as they connect the church or ministry to experts who can add value to the planning process.

Prayerful boards ask God to provide wise counselors to guide the planning process.

Help this board avoid the herd mentality that could stampede the ministry in a dangerous and reckless direction.

Southern Alberta Canada is home to Head-Smashed-In Buffalo Jump Provincial Park. Quite a name – quite a story. In short, the indigenous Blackfeet Indians depended upon the bison for food, used their hides for blankets, and their horns for tools. They would masquerade as wolves to approach and startle a herd of bison grazing in the area. The Indians would stampede the terrified animals toward a nearby cliff, frightening the poor beasts over the edge and to their untimely demise.

The challenge was the lead buffalo. If they succeeded in racing the first buffalo over the cliff, the rest of the herd would follow. The *herd mentality* was deadly for the buffalo of Alberta, and it can be destructive for boards today.

Unchallenged, a powerful board member can lead the willing herd of board members in a perilous direction. Open discussion, spirited debate, and thorough questioning are not bad things. They are essential for healthy boards and help reduce the risk of a run-away board.

Create a culture of open discussion. Encourage pushback. Ask members to point out weaknesses in the plan. Ask, "How can we make this better?" The chair should remind the board members to maintain an attitude of discovery in an atmosphere of grace. The goal is to discern God's will, not promote a personal agenda. Board members should not strive to dominate a discussion or win an argument, rather they should work to discern God's plan for the institution.

Design brake-tapping elements within the board systems and structure. A friend says, "Never throw raw meat on the board table." We need to let ideas marinate and slow cook to ensure that the entrée is prepared just right. Committees provide opportunities for ideas to be challenged and refined before they go to the entire board. New and possibly divisive ideas should be allowed to simmer so that areas of concern can emerge and be addressed. Committees tend to slow down the process, but they help boards respond cautiously to difficult and dangerous challenges rather than with knee-jerk and hazardous reactions.

Recruit board members who have faced bigger challenges than the organization will ever address. People who have supervised budgets ten times the size of your church or ministry will likely be unthreatened by the size of your church or ministries challenges. People who have managed large organizations will be less threatened by HR concerns from a staff of ten. Board members who have faced and overcome major life challenges will be well equipped to address the painful and complex issues that face most churches and nonprofits.

Never compromise when considering the spiritual maturity of new board members. But spiritual maturity should be coupled with life skills and leadership experience. Candidates who have never faced high-dollar, high-stakes decisions are often intimidated and unprepared for the challenges of ministry leadership. Those who have addressed big, tough decisions or withstood painful life challenges may be less easily spooked by large problems and more likely to avoid running with the herd in a harmful direction.

PRAYERFUL BOARDS

Prayerful boards create systems to minimize risk and avoid quick and disastrous decisions.

H elp us see which decisions are easily reversed and which ones are changed at great peril.

The herd mentality we just examined is most destructive in decisions that are difficult to correct. The lead buffalo can run anywhere it wants with little consequence, until it encounters a cliff. The three big cliffs where boards need special caution are *staffing*, *debt*, and *construction*.

Hiring a new pastor or CEO is arguably the most significant task any board will face. If the board gets that decision right, every other challenge will be much easier. Selecting new members of the board is also critically important. Prayerful, cautious, and wise discernment is needed in these key decisions. Paul warns Timothy to be cautious and take his time filling leadership positions. He tells Timothy, *Do not be hasty in the laying on of hands* (1 Timothy 5:22a). It is much less painful for a board *not to hire* a pastor or CEO or *not to invite* a candidate for board membership than it is to deal with conflict, division, and turmoil for years.

Issuing debt encumbers the ministry for years to come, often past the point that any board members who approved the debt still sit on the board. Every church and nonprofit board must wrestle with policies concerning *if, when,* and *why* to issue debt. The reality remains that this is a long-term obligation that will influence other decisions for the length of the note. Boards should consider well the debt's impact upon the ministry in the days and years to come.

Construction is another area where *go-slow* is appropriate. Before workers begin chopping down trees or pouring concrete, aesthetics, sight lines, and architectural congruency should be addressed. But greater than these issues are the questions of *highest and best use.* Is this the best spot for the new educational building? Do we really need a new library now that most books are available electronically? What else might be placed in this location? Whether a church, school, camp, or homeless shelter, every new building or major addition, should fit into a master facility plan to avoid costly and embarrassing removal and relocation issues five, ten, or twenty years down the road.

Measure twice cut once is good advice for builders, but crucial advice for boards. Avoiding *paralysis by analysis* is certainly important, but more damage is done in haste than by taking a second look. Discuss the issue until everyone has received adequate input, questions have been sufficiently addressed, and all board members are willing to live with the results.

PRAYERFUL BOARDS

Prayerful boards take their time when making decisions with long-term implications.

Personal Reflections

Are you better at accurately assessing the internal issues (condition of the ship), or analyzing the context within which the ministry operates (the weather report)?

Are there any long-time traditions that you are unwilling to jettison even though they are not as effective as in the past? What should you do going forward?

How do you respond to a strong leader? With compliance and allegiance, with resistance and defiance, or with cautious and well-founded trust?

Can you recall a time when you followed a leader in an unwise direction?

Board Discussion

How does planning happen within your board? Is it primarily vision casting or vision discovery?

How much time does the board spend assessing the internal workings of the ministry (condition of the ship), and how much is invested in analyzing the ministry context (the weather report)? Is this the best balance? How should things change?

What aspect of your ministry is being retained because of its effectiveness years ago? How should you proceed?

Does your board suffer from the seduction of the herd? Is there a dangerous direction that should be addressed and avoided?

CHAPTER 7

REMAIN UNIFIED

And dear God, help us remain unified.

While in Kenya, teaching a group of eager, committed, and creative Christian camping leaders, I used a very American expression. I said, "How do you eat an elephant?" I expected the group to respond, "One bite at a time!" Instead, I saw nothing but blank stares. I knew I had missed my audience, so I forged ahead in a new direction.

After the seminar, one courageous student approached me and said, "If you have an elephant to eat, you should call the whole village."

I've *chewed* on that response for a long time. In the West, we honor independence and personal accomplishment. We want to do it all by ourselves. In Africa, and in many other cultures, community support and cooperation are expected.

Board work is community work. Boards succeed or fail together. Unity is essential. We cannot *eat the elephant* all by ourselves. We must cooperate and depend upon our colleagues on the board to accomplish the great thing God has placed before the church or ministry organization.

I find it significant that the *Greatest Commandment* comes before the *Great Commission*. Jesus explains how to *treat* people before he shares what we are to *tell* them! He places his expectation for our *attitudes* before his admonition for our *actions*.

Matthew, a reformed tax-collector, records the dialogue between Jesus and a crafty attorney who tried to box him into a theological and political corner.

> *One of them, an expert in the law, tested him with this question: "Teacher, which is the greatest commandment in the Law?" Jesus replied: "'Love the Lord your God with all your heart and with all your soul and with all your mind.' This is the first and greatest commandment. And the second is like it: 'Love your neighbor as yourself.' All the Law and the Prophets hang on these two commandments."* (Matthew 22:35-40)

Expressing our love for God and for others is clearly instructed. Loving God and those around us is a bedrock demonstration of our faith. Not only are we commanded to love God and others, but we are also commissioned to *make disciples*. A few chapters after Matthew records the

Greatest Commandment, he records the *Great Commission.* With his last earthly words Jesus gives us our marching orders.

> *Then Jesus came to them and said, "All authority in heaven and on earth has been given to me. Therefore go and make disciples of all nations, baptizing them in the name of the Father and of the Son and of the Holy Spirit, and teaching them to obey everything I have commanded you. And surely I am with you always, to the very end of the age."* (Matthew 28:18-20)

To produce more than wood, hay, and stubble, our actions must be motivated by a heart of love. Both *love* and *service* are expected – but love comes first. Authentic works for God never originate from sinful motives. For those who follow Christ, the end never justifies inappropriate means.

The Corinthian Church was filled with divisions, dissension, sin, and turmoil. Paul addresses their behavior but gives them the ultimate solution in chapter 13. This passage on love is often read at weddings, and that is fine. But it was originally read in the tough times of discord and tension as a reminder of our high calling. We must love well to reflect Christ accurately to a needy world. Paul reminds the Corinthians and us:

> *If I speak in the tongues of men and of angels, but have not love, I am only a resounding gong or a clanging cymbal. If I have the gift of prophecy and can fathom all mysteries and all knowledge, and if I have a faith that can move mountains, but have not love, I am nothing. If I give all I possess to the poor and surrender my body to the flames, but have not love, I gain nothing.* (1 Corinthians 13:1-3)

Boards strive to align their church or ministry's efforts with the fulfillment of the *Great Commission.* Whatever the form, the *work* must be done in *ways* that maintain the loving unity derived from obeying the *Greatest Command-ment*. Unity of *motive* and unity of *mission* are achieved as boards *love well* and *work well*, striving together.

Prayerful boards love well and serve well.

A llow every member to express his or her opinion fully.

A boisterous or powerful board member may easily control discussion and manipulate ill-informed, intimidated, or uninitiated board members. Consent agendas, closed committee work, and limited access to information can all disrupt honest and open deliberations.

Consent agendas save time and expedite meetings. This procedure groups several smaller, perfunctory issues into one package that is voted on with a consolidated motion. Grouping multiple issues that require little discussion into a single action item is prudent. However, board members should retain the prerogative to pull any item out of the package for deeper discussion. The goal of a consent agenda is to expedite routine matters and to allocate more time to deeper discussions on issues of greater significance. A consent agenda should not be used to hide messy problems or to avoid uncomfortable discussions.

Board committees exist to help the full board do its work more efficiently. Finance committees, nominating committees, program committees, and performance review committees are common within many boards. But committees merely study issues, do research, and prepare recommendations for the full board's deliberation. The entire board should hear adequate, relevant, and clear information to make informed decisions.

Members, especially new members, may feel overwhelmed and intimidated by the operational machinery of the board as it churns. The chair, and other senior members, should take care to help expedite the learning curves of new members. Training events, board mentors, and timely reports can help bring everyone up to speed.

The greatest risk, however, is not consent agendas, committees, on-boarding of new members, or any other operational strategy; the greatest risk is *power*. To avoid the appearance or reality of a power-play and to facilitate long-term unity, boards should ensure that there is a consensus on two simple statements before a vote is taken. Everyone should affirm that:

- The issue has been thoroughly discussed, and all questions have been asked and answered adequately.
- Everyone has had a fair opportunity to participate in the discussion. All members of the board have had ample time and adequate information to engage in the deliberation process.

Responsible board chairs encourage open and thoughtful input from every member. They allow appropriate discussion time to ensure that every member has the opportunity to form and express their opinion.

Prayerful boards speak openly and honestly.

Help us engage the dreams for the future with harmony and enthusiasm.

Board work is ultimately about the future. Boards should retain an adequate knowledge of the past and a clear assessment of the present to lead their organizations into *better futures*. Boards *evaluate* the past, *engage in* the present, and *envision* the future.

Often the pastor or CEO is the first to discern the future that the Lord has in store for the church or nonprofit organization. Sometimes it is a senior board member, a long-term staff member, or a major donor who glimpses the future. There is no limit to the techniques God may use to make his plans known. However, the plan must gain the support of the board if it hopes to reach full bloom.

Generally, dreams of a better future emerge at the intersection of three fundamental arenas. The *ministry's strengths*, the *beneficiaries' needs*, and the *necessary resources*.

First, every church and nonprofit ministry is filled with staff and volunteers with special skills, interests, passions, knowledge, and desires. Leadership staff and board members should become aware of the strengths and weaknesses within the institution. Focusing on strengths, building upon what the ministry already does well, and harnessing the passion that currently exists, fast tracks broad support.

Second, the beneficiaries and their needs must be clearly defined. Needs are plentiful, but organizations have limits. God has not called any of us to do it all, but he has called all of us to do our part. We must focus our efforts to *accomplish more by doing less*. Feeding the homeless in Chicago. Educating elementary age children in Louisville. Drilling water-wells in Zambia. Or starting a satellite church in Tacoma. Each envisions a better future but also limits the scope and geography of the challenges. The more precisely the church or ministry can define *who* it is striving to serve and *what* they hope to accomplish, the more unified and focused the board's efforts will be.

Third, ministries need resources to operate: people, money, equipment, licenses, materials, education, certification, and a host of related items. Only God operates without limits. Fortunately, even though resources are *limited*, they are also *elastic*. We can raise more money, recruit more volunteers, gain more education, and enlist more prayer warriors. Working together to expand resources and increase the impact of the church or nonprofit can energize and unify the board, staff, donors, volunteers and every stakeholder in the organization.

It is crucial to prayerfully explore and discern God's direction. The plan for the future of a church or ministry is often discovered at the intersection of strengths, beneficiaries, and resources.

*Prayerful boards stay unified as they discern
the next step God has for their ministry.*

Help each of us leave this meeting with the commitment to speak with one voice and support the group decisions in public and private.

The role of the board chair or an appointed board spokesperson is crucial. The agreed upon outcomes of a challenging meeting can quickly splinter into numerous versions of the same story, each with a slightly different emphasis filtering into the various constituent groups. Intentionally or not, we all have our own slant on the events that transpired.

After twelve years of suffering Jesus healed a woman. Luke, a physician, recounts the circumstances leading up to Jesus' miracle. He says, *And a woman was there who had been subject to bleeding for twelve years, but no one could heal her* (Luke 8:43).

Mark's account explains the same event, but with a little different attitude. Apparently, Mark was no friend of doctors. He records, *She had suffered a great deal under the care of many doctors and had spent all she had, yet instead of getting better she grew worse* (Mark 5:26).

The physician, Dr. Luke, recounts the same story as Mark, but the two descriptions portray the medical world in very different lights. Different reports of the same event are always filtered through the lens of our personal biases. It happened in the Bible, and it happens with boards.

No matter how objective we may try to be, our biases will emerge. One person should speak for the group, especially regarding difficult or complex issues. Most decisions are routine and comfortable, free from discord. Few topics are all that sensitive, but some actions can be painful or divisive. A written statement that precisely articulates the board's collective position may be the best way to address issues of great concern. The one-voice process helps board members remain unified.

Assuming the deliberation was open, fair, and all perspectives have been aired thoroughly, some general comments from board members can help reassure stakeholders of the integrity of the process. Statements such as these are usually quite appropriate:

- We prayed hard, wrestled with many ideas, and looked at several alternatives. This plan is not going to please everyone, but we think this is the path God is leading us.
- I appreciate the time the board members put into studying this issue and examining the various options. Please continue to pray for the ministry as we implement this significant decision.

- This was one of the hardest decisions we have had to make. I'm very glad we were able to prayerfully develop a plan that will guide us going forward.

Private conversations, even with a spouse, can violate the trust of the board. Err on the side of caution. When a board member shares confidential information outside of the board context, he or she usually asks that person to keep the details to themselves. Ironically, the board member is expecting the person receiving the nugget of information to do what he or she could not. A board member who shares confidential information is asking the friend or relative to bear a burden he or she was unwilling or unable to carry. Besides ethical considerations, legal issues may arise in some circumstances.

Prayerful boards speak with one voice, in public and private conversations.

Help us remember that few decisions are worth the divisions caused by dominant winning or belligerent losing.

I have often wondered if competition entered the human experience before or after sin reared its ugly head. There are some benefits gained, and values instilled through competition, but dark forces lurk just below the surface of many competitive events. Winning and losing are parts of life, and we need to do both well. But not every decision within a board meeting needs to be competitive.

Governments draft legislation within a highly competitive arena. Striving to garner enough votes to win is a daily battle. But in church and nonprofit ministry contexts, the process need not be contentious. Jesus said, *By this all men will know that you are my disciples, if you love one another* (John 13:35). Notice, he did not say that the world would be impressed by our brilliant insights, powerful decisions, detailed plans, or pithy comments. *Love* should be the ultimate core value of every Christ follower.

In the grand scheme of things, *how* we win and lose is more significant than *if* we win or lose:

- Do we love winning more than we love the board members whose opinions differ from ours?
- Do we love them enough to offer congratulations if our ideas go down in flames while their plans are approved?
- Do we love them enough to express sincere appreciation for dissenting proposals?
- Do we work to modify our plans to accommodate minority positions, even though we have the votes to win?

Keeping score is also counterproductive. Payback for hurt feelings and reprisals for past offenses are cancers that can destroy the soul of any board. Each decision should be viewed as an on-ramp to the next challenge, not an end in itself. The work of the board is always twofold, on one hand, to find the best way forward for the organization, and on the other, to make those decisions in God-honoring ways.

Prayerful boards love each other more than winning.

Help us seek your glory and not ours.

I have vivid memories from my early childhood of my dad inviting me to help him build a small porch on the back of a rental house our family owned. I spent most of a sunny Saturday picking up scrap boards, handing him nails, holding the end of a tape measure, and steadying a board while he sawed. At the end of the day, *we* looked with great satisfaction at the porch *we* had made. The work probably took him a little longer with my help, but dad allowed me the privilege of working with him on a project I could never have accomplished myself.

My childhood porch-building experience was not unlike board work. God allows us to participate with him to accomplish things that we could never do on our own. So, who gets the credit? Who gets the praise? Who gets the honor when things go well?

When we seek the glory, take the credit, and expect to be honored for our contributions, we demonstrate that we have forgotten *Whose* ministry it is and *Who* should receive the glory.

Celebrations are important. We should feel joy over accomplishments and sense satisfaction from projects that reach a successful conclusion. But *who* and *what* we celebrate are key. We must never lose focus on the object of our joy, the One who designed the plan, provided the resources, and allowed us to participate in the work with him.

Many churches sing the Doxology as an entrance to their worship services. The Doxology begins, *Praise God from whom all blessings flow*. That is a simple yet powerful reminder to give credit where credit is due. As we sing those words, we remind ourselves that God is the source of the blessings we enjoy. In those moments, we genuinely thank God for his provision. But once the last *Amen* is sung, we file out of the church building, drive home, and eventually gather at the board table. The lyrics may be quickly forgotten, and we return to our well-worn patterns of worry, strife, and conflict.

Paul reminded the Corinthians of the importance of remaining focused on glorifying God in every area of our lives. *So whether you eat or drink or whatever you do, do it all for the glory of God* (1 Corinthians 10:31). The *whatever you do* includes board meetings.

Prayerful boards give God the glory.

Grant us the joy of arriving at adjournment closer to one another because we are closer to you.

Congruency with God's design is the ultimate source of joy. Walking step-by-step with him does not make life easier, but it does make each day a thrilling adventure. Walking with him gets us past the win-lose drama and through the pain, fears, and disappointments of life. Aligning with his plan helps us focus on *how* more than *what*, and *Who* more than *anything*.

When boards are doing God's work God's way, the result should be both a deep sense of joy and a powerful bond of unity.

Tyler, Texas, grows lots and lots of roses. The growers ship rose bushes to nurseries throughout the country and beyond. Before the plants are shipped, the buds are clipped, gathered, bundled, and sold. A dozen roses can be purchased for a few dollars at many stops throughout the city. The beautiful blooms are not the point; they are the byproduct. While growing and selling the bushes is the goal, the roses produce a magnificent byproduct – gorgeous flowers that add value and beauty. In a small way, the roses are like board work.

The men and women who sit around the table shoulder the responsibility to tend the garden. They care for the rosebushes, prune and plant, endure the thorns, and pray the garden grows. They do not serve with the goal of developing deep relationships and establishing life-long friendships, but that is often the *glorious byproduct*.

Working hard with other like-minded believers, wrestling through tough decisions, weighing the risks and rewards, and struggling to discern God's direction for the ministry all produce the twin byproducts of a closer relationship with God and a closer relationship with the brothers and sisters with whom board members share those experiences.

Doing God's work and doing it in God-honoring ways is a reward in itself. But the byproducts, a sense of God's approval and a closeness with others are benefits *above what we could ask or think.*

PRAYERFUL BOARDS

Prayerful boards lock arms, accomplish the great thing God has called them to do, and enjoy the blessings of good and faithful servants.

A men.

Personal Reflections

In your board service, do you tend to emphasize obeying the Greatest Commandment or fulfilling the Great Commission?

Remember your first board meeting. How did you feel? What did the veteran board members do to make you feel included?

What special contribution do you make to the board deliberations? What unique perspective or experience do you add to the discussion?

What beneficial by-products have you experienced due to your time in board service?

Board Discussion

What can your board do in the recruiting process, the onboarding experience, and the initial
board meetings to make new board members feel
included and valued?

Are there ways your board can ensure that all members feel fully included and respectfully heard?

How do you feel about the board policy concerning
sharing confidential deliberations outside of the
boardroom? Are there any changes needed?

Do we generally feel good about our relationships
with one another, and with God, when our meetings
end? What can be done to improve these relationships?

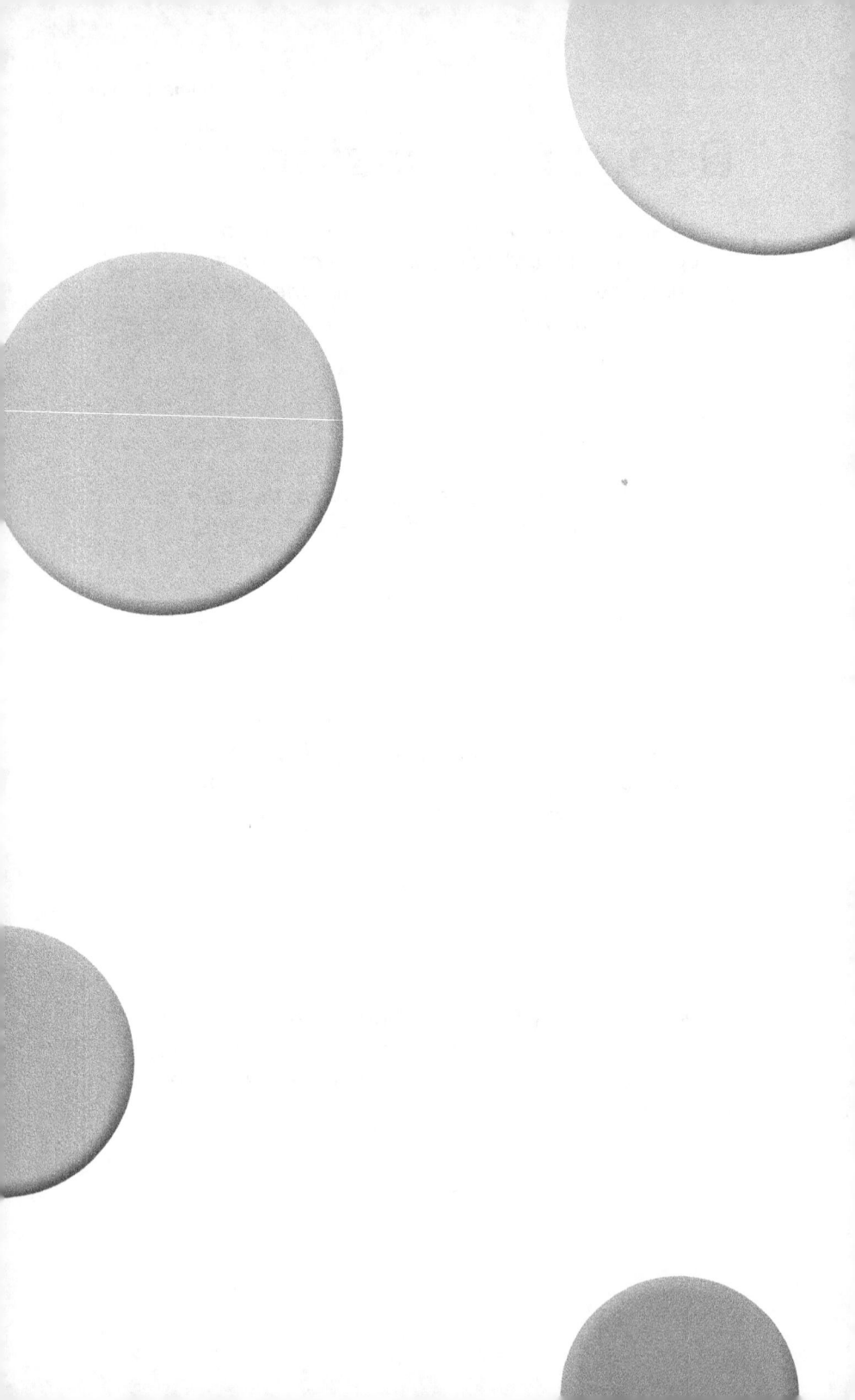

APPENDIX

A Board Prayer
by Dr. Dan Bolin

Dear God, thank you.

- Thank you for calling this ministry into existence and for allowing it to serve and care for the people you love.

- Thank you for the various perspectives represented in this meeting and the things we will learn from one another.

- Thank you for the privilege of corporately receiving reports, and with one voice establishing policies, discovering direction, setting goals, and encouraging those who serve in this ministry.

- Thank you for the many people whose lives will be influenced through our meeting - other board members, staff, volunteers, donors, participants, vendors, and generations yet unborn who will benefit from the decisions we make today.

- And God, thank you for entrusting your ministry into our care. Help us be worthy of the trust that you and others are placing in us.

Father, allow me to report honestly.

- Help me tell the whole truth, not just the parts that make me look good.

- Let me not bury bad news in mounds of data and detail, and don't let me gloss over painful issues or personal failures.

- Help me give credit to others and take responsibility for failure and lack of progress.

- Don't let me trivialize serious issues or magnify minor successes.

- Let me tell stories and provide statistics that represent accurately.

- Help me remember that good information provides a smooth pathway to good decisions.

God, as we approach this meeting, help us see clearly.

- Help us see the issues before us from many perspectives - but ultimately from your perspective. Align our thoughts with your thoughts and our work with your desire.

- God, help us see our ministry's strengths and weaknesses and embrace both.

- Help us connect the dots between the many good ideas to find the great idea you have for us.

- Help us distinguish what is significant from what is superficial, what is short-term from what is long-term, and what is best for me from what is best for all.

Help me listen objectively.

- Allow me the grace to filter angry words and hear the truth behind what is being said.

- Help me listen to the painful heart from which flows harsh comments.

- Help me learn from what is legitimate and discard what is said in spite.

- Help me respond to questions with grace and respect.

- Allow me to focus on what is being said more than how I will respond.

Help me **speak cautiously.**

- Let me use the fewest words, the least intensity, and the lowest volume needed to be understood.

- Help me voice my opinions with care, strength, and meekness.

- Help me ask good questions, open dialogue, explore options, and deepen discussion.

- Help me say nothing degrading and nothing that would draw lines of conflict unnecessarily.

- Help me affirm and agree whenever possible.

- Help me give second-voice to a courageous and wise first-voice; those who risk presenting a new, contrary, or unrefined perspective.

- Lord, help me accept compliments and approval with humility.

- God, give me the grace to watch with dignity as my proposal fails, and give me humility when my idea meets with approval.

Dear God, give the board wisdom to **plan wisely.**

- Help us see opportunities and threats and count the cost as we weigh risks and rewards.

- Help us see the possibilities for a better future.

- Help us honor the past and give us the courage to abandon the methods that provided yesterday's success but will lead to futility tomorrow.

- Help us discover and employ the most effective methods to accomplish your mission for this ministry in the days ahead.

- Help this board avoid the herd mentality that could stampede the ministry in a dangerous and reckless direction.

- Help us see which decisions are easily reversed and which ones are changed at great peril.

And Dear God, help us remain unified.

- Allow every member to express his or her opinion fully.

- Help us engage the dreams for the future with harmony and enthusiasm.

- Help each of us leave this meeting with the commitment to speak with one voice and support the group decisions in public and private.

- Help us remember that few decisions are worth the divisions caused by dominant winning or belligerent losing.

- Help us seek your glory and not ours.

- Grant us the joy of arriving at adjournment closer to one another because we are closer to you.

Amen.

Scan for free printable version of **A Board Prayer**
www.refuelinginflight.com/boardprayer

Interested in Dan speaking with your board?
Contact us at info@refuelinginflight.com

Backstory, Benefits, and Application

During my high school years, I enjoyed journalism, history, and English. I had a good time in gym class and study hall, but I stayed a long way away from classes involving numbers. I appreciated being a teacher's aide in journalism and loved my year as the sports editor of the newspaper. But my anchor class in high school was student government. Besides planning and organizing events, we studied *Robert's Rules of Order*, basic government, leadership, and organizational theory.

A few years ago, I found a notebook with the documents from rewriting the Roosevelt High School Student Government Constitution in 1968. Looking at that binder I realized I'd repeated that process with three nonprofit organizations during my career. Maybe I learned everything I needed to know in my high school student government class.

After college I went to work for Pine Cove Christian Camps. There I was introduced to board governance and learned from some of the best. Phil Hook, the executive director, invited me to attend many of the board meetings. They were educational, interesting, and at times entertaining, but when they ended, I went back to work. I focused on my routines and responsibilities, developing meaningful camp ministry experiences for second through sixth graders. Eight years, one wife, one daughter, one house, and one seminary degree later, I found myself as the executive director. My view of the board from that vantage point was significantly different. I began to see the work of board governance in a whole new light.

Over the next fourteen years I served as the executive director of Pine Cove. Following that I was honored to become the president of the Educational Radio Foundation of East Texas – KVNE/KGLY. After nine years in that role, I moved on to head Christian Camping International, a coalition of more than two-dozen national and regional associations serving millions of campers and staff in over sixty countries. For over 30 years, healthy board relationships were vital to my effectiveness and crucial to the success and failure of each institution.

Along the way I sat on local, regional, national, and international nonprofit boards. I served on my church's elder board and was elected to a seat on our local school board where I served for seven years. Within the nonprofit world, I have worked *for* boards and served *on* boards for a long time and seen boards at their best - and at their worst.

Genesis of the Prayer

While leading Christian Camping International, we held one of our annual board meetings in Bangalore, India. Members from Australia, Colombia, Kenya, Netherlands, New Zealand, Russia, South Africa, UK, and USA were in the room. The group was diverse geographically, politically, racially, economically, linguistically, and sociologically. But each of the members shared a strong commitment to the Lord and deeply desired to see the expansion, networking, and cooperation of Christian camping around the world.

As sure as winter follows autumn, the time arrived for my annual performance review. As was our practice, I was asked to step out of the room. The small committee that had met with me earlier to evaluate my year's performance in detail, briefed the full board outside my presence. I sat down the hall in a small, secluded waiting area expecting a short moment in solitude. However, my short wait seemed like it was taking a long time.

The longer I waited, the more my mind wandered toward preposterous scenarios. *Had I offended someone? Had I committed a cultural taboo? Had I missed something in my committee's review?*

To fill the moment and keep my mind occupied, I started to pray and write. I often write to crystallize, clarify, and organize my thoughts. The result of that break in my busy schedule is *A Board Prayer.* I polished and rewrote it numerous times. As Justice Louis Brandeis said, "There are no great writers – only great rewriters." But the heart of the *Prayer*, and most of the verbiage, emerged during that brief hiatus in the hallway of a small mission house in India.

After almost an hour, the board realized that I was still in the hall. My review had been short and sweet. But they had engaged in a lively discussion and neglected to open the door and invite me back into the room. *All's well that ends well* and the *Prayer* was birthed.

Maintaining both ministry and personal lives can be complex. So, years ago, I established a small nonprofit to manage the time and money related to ministry opportunities outside of my official responsibilities. Today, Refueling in Flight Ministries (RIF) provides the structure and support that I need to write, teach, speak, and share what I have learned. I cannot escape; I still work for a board!

The RIF Board consists of my wife, myself, and three dear friends. They know me well enough, and we have been friends long enough, for them to tell me the truth. Their advice, counsel, questions, and affirmation has been invaluable. Besides the wisdom they provide to establish direction and to focus the resources of RIF, the byproduct has been the extended and deepened relationship we share. They will be my pallbearers.

Boards are that way. The corporate effort can generate a relational bond that is deep and rich.

Working for boards and serving on boards I made more than my fair share of mistakes. However, I am proud of most of my decisions. Whether wise or foolish, good or bad, simple or complex, I learned from all of them. The reflections in this little book come from the insights gleaned during the highs and lows of those experiences. And I pray that these thoughts will help guide church and nonprofit boards into greater effectiveness, deeper relationships and more God-honoring practices.

In full disclosure, the stories in this book are all true. However, the people, places, and times of some accounts have been altered to shield those involved without losing the significance of the illustrations.

Building a God-Honoring Board

Boards are (or should be) filled with people who have demonstrated their ability to make good corporate decisions. However, successful people in the business arena may or may not be spiritually qualified to lead a church or a nonprofit ministry, even if they have signed the statement of faith. Paul warns Timothy about the serious downside of capricious leadership decisions. He says, *Do not be hasty in the laying on of hands* (1 Timothy 5:22a). We often think, "Why slow down the process? Either the candidate can read a balance sheet, or not."

What takes time to discern is not their ability to make corporate decisions, that is easily discoverable. What takes a little longer is the *how*. *How* do they relate to people? *How* do they respond to conflict? *How* do they fit into a team? *How* will they react if they are not the smartest person in the room?

A few verses later, Paul continues his instruction to young Timothy. He says, *The sins of some men are obvious, reaching the place of judgment ahead of them; the sins of others trail behind them* (1 Timothy 5:24). We can never know the depths of any person's heart, and we are all susceptible to making sinful mistakes. But the recent past is the best predictor of the future. Taking the time to get to know a person's heart, before inviting him or her to serve on the board, is critical to the health of any church or ministry organization.

Many of the lessons shared in *A Board Prayer* flow from some hasty decisions to invite new members to the board. My assumptions about people with exceptional resumes, impressive contact lists, and large bank accounts blurred my vision. I made several hasty decisions I wish I could redo, but a card laid is a card played! Samuel read the resume of David's older brother and was ready to anoint him the next king of Israel. But God's leadership selection process is more rigorous than ours.

But the LORD said to Samuel, "Do not consider his appearance or his height, for I have rejected him. The LORD does not look at the things man looks at. Man looks at the outward appearance, but the LORD looks at the heart." (1 Samuel 16:7)

Do not relax the spiritual and relational standards of the church or nonprofit to enlist an intriguing potential board member. The organizational abilities and financial insights that a potential new member may bring to the boardroom are critical. Every ministry needs to make wise and strategic corporate decisions. But when you go fishing for new members, only go to a pond that is filled with people whose hearts are committed to the Lord, who have a track record of loving and serving others, and who seek the best possible outcomes in difficult situations.

Who Benefits?

There are many ways to organize and operate governing boards. Some structures and practices are better than others. All churches and nonprofit organizations wrestle with many *how-to* issues of board governance. This book is not a textbook explaining how to improve, streamline, or reorganize a board. It is not an *operating manual* full of how-to ideas and fresh governance tactics, rather is it an *insight manual* encouraging boards to glorify God in the way they do what they do. It contains a little help on how to lead and manage churches and ministries, but that is not the foremost intent.

This book is primarily about helping board members, and those who interact directly with boards, discover and implement God-honoring governance practices. It is about boards working in ways that please God and that reflect the values Christian churches and institutions espouse. These principles apply no matter what style of board governance a church or ministry may employ.

Churches and nonprofit organizations use an array of names for the governing body that makes ownership style decisions: vestry, session, elders, deacons, trustees, board, and I'm sure there are others I have missed. For ease of communication, I have generally used the word *board* to describe the group holding the highest level of authority within the organization.

I pray that two groups benefit directly from this book, and a third party indirectly. *First*, I hope that board members are the primary beneficiaries. Tens of thousands of volunteers serve honorably on church and nonprofit boards. The vast majority do so with little training and minimal support. I hope the pages of *A Board Prayer* resonate with these loyal leaders and provide encouragement and insight. Following closely is a *second* group of pastors, CEOs, and other key leadership staff who interface with church and nonprofit boards. This group benefits most from the marvelous joys of good governance, and they feel the deepest pain from harsh, foolish, and ignoble board actions. I hope this group finds ways to influence their leaders into more effective practices. *Third*, and possibly most importantly, I hope the parishioners, clients, staff members, volunteers, donors, vendors, and others associated with churches and nonprofits also benefit.

Applying *A* Board Prayer

The *Prayer* has been used in a variety of ways. Some boards pray it together at the start of each meeting. Some pray it silently and then share ideas and commitments their meditation has inspired. Some share it around the table with board members reading sequential lines. Others read one section at various breaks in the meeting schedule. Some encourage each member to read it ahead of their meetings to prepare their souls for the work ahead. Others use it annually rather than employing it at each gathering.

Two sets of questions follow each chapter. The first group guides the reader into a time of self-reflection. The second questions are designed to stimulate discussion within the board to explore better pathways forward.

The *Prayer* is copyrighted to control the content, not to impede its availability. It felt strange claiming ownership to a prayer. I want it prayed and used, but I also want to be responsible only for the original version, not modified editions with unsanctioned changes. But feel free to share *this version* of *A Board Prayer* as you like.

Whatever the application of the *Prayer*, help your board find a way to resonate with the heart of the message. Make *A Board Prayer*, your prayer and align your hearts with God's heart. Then go to work accomplishing that great thing that God has put before you.

Acknowledgments

To properly acknowledge the many people who helped develop and capture the concepts in this book would take another book. But failing to recognize a few of the key contributors would be a greater injustice.

Let me begin with the current board members of Refueling in Flight Ministries. Bedford Holmes, Ken Sutterfield, Brad Mercer, and my wife Cay Bolin all provide direction, support, wise counsel, and affirmation. Several years ago they pushed me to put my thoughts on paper and encouraged me to share them with a broader audience.

Lori Price, my assistant, contributed countless hours reading, rereading, and scouring this manuscript. She provided the graphic design work and pushed me to rethink and re-craft numerous mushy or redundant paragraphs. Marty Putman, who served as my assistant before Lori, helped shape the original version of this *Prayer*. Her fingerprints remain from that initial input.

Carol Crawford raised the bar. Her keen editorial eye, professional writing experience, and gracious guidance helped refine this project and shape the final outcome. You encountered only about 40% of my original semi-colons and exclamation points; due to her excellent work!

Several institutions and ministries have utilized and helped circulate the original version of the *Prayer*. InterVarsity, Evangelical Council for Financial Accountability, Thriving Boards Initiative of the Murdock Trust, Christian Camping International, Camp Tejas, and many more.

I would be remiss to not mention a few significant trainers and mentors who poured their wisdom and knowledge into my board experiences. John Pearson, Bob Andringa, Don Goehner, Bob Buford, Phil Hook, Bob Kobielush, Jim Fletemeyer, Jim Halls, Fred Miller, and Bob Kraning. Most of these are now in Glory, I hope they can see the fruit of their labor.

No list could capture the full complement of board members for whom I worked or with whom I served alongside. Besides John Harper, Brenda Cagle, and Lorimer Gray, who I mentioned in the dedication, I would like to recognize a very few board members whose godly examples and profound wisdom helped shape my thinking and contributed to the concepts in this book: Alexander Kharitonov, Bruce Dunning, Newt Farrar, Paul Glaske, Wally Anderson, Eldon Steele, Huel Weaver, Jeff Strout, Tom Ramey Jr., Pat Thomas, and Don Hanley. Many of these great board members have departed this life. Their influence, however, continues.

Several readers took an early peek at the project and shared much needed encouragement and endorsements. I am indebted to Alec Hill, April Moreton, Michael Martin, Richard Dahlstrom, Fred Smith, Paul Biles, Wayne Braudrick, Bob Kobielush, Ron Marrs, Tom Nisbett, Linda Paulk, Lorin Roncancio, and Ray Schnickles.

Finally, I want to thank my wife Cay who not only serves on the Refueling in Flight Ministries board, but listens to my ramblings, asks pointed questions, and spells words correctly from across the room. She has completed numerous Bible studies, while sitting next to me in dozens of coffee shops around the world as I tried to weave a tangle of ideas into seven helpful strands that we now know as *A Board Prayer*.

A bout the Author

Dr. Dan Bolin is an author, teacher, and ministry leader dedicated to helping Christian leaders serve with wisdom, humility, and grace. As President of Refueling in Flight Ministries, he encourages pastors, board members, and nonprofit leaders around the world to lead in ways that honor God and strengthen His people.

With more than forty years of experience in Christian leadership, Dr. Bolin has served as International Director of Christian Camping International, President of KVNE/KGLY Christian Radio, and Executive Director of Pine Cove Christian Camps. His extensive background also includes teaching, consulting, and speaking engagements in over thirty countries, where he has guided ministries in leadership development, strategic planning, and board governance.

Dr. Bolin holds a Doctor of Ministry from Denver Seminary, a Master of Business Administration from LeTourneau University, and a Master of Theology from Dallas Theological Seminary. He is the author of numerous books, including Blueprints, Jesus: Camp Director, and A Board Prayer.

Dan and his wife, Cay, make their home in Culpeper, Virginia, where they enjoy time with their family, grandchildren, and the beauty of God's creation.

To receive weekly devotions and ministry updates, subscribe: www.refuelinginflight.com/subscribe

About Refueling in Flight Ministries

Refueling in Flight Ministries exists to encourage, assist, and connect Christian ministry leaders, especially camping leaders, in the United States and around the world. This is done through:

- **Writing** - weekly devotions, periodic blogs, and books.
- **Teaching** - in academic settings, professional training events, and churches.
- **Connecting** - through CEO Dialogues, international relationships, and retreats.

Refueling in Flight is a 501c3 tax-exempt organization. For more details go to www.refuelinginflight.com.

Other Works by the Author

October Storm
Lessons Learned on Pain, Loss, Gratitude, and Joy
RIF Publishing – 2024

Jesus: Camp Director
5,000 Campers, 12 Interns, and 0 Kitchen Staff
RIF Publishing – 2023 (also available in Spanish)

Blueprints
Biblical Designs for Christian Camping: Yesterday, Today and Tomorrow
RIF Publishing – 2022 (also available in Spanish and Italian)

Fresh Bread Devotions
Self-Published – 2016

The Winning Run and Other Life Lessons from Baseball
with Ed Diaz | NavPress – 1999

A Hole in One and Other Life Lessons from Golf
NavPress – 1999

Avoiding the Blitz and Other Life Lessons from Football
NavPress – 1998

The One that Got Away and Other Life Lessons from Fishing
NavPress – 1998

How to Be Your Wife's Best Friend
with John Trent | NavPress – 1994

How to Be Your Little Man's Dad
with Ken Sutterfield | NavPress – 1993

How to Be Your Daughter's Daddy
NavPress – 1993

About John Pearson

John Pearson, a board governance consultant, served 30 years as a nonprofit CEO, including 25 years as CEO of three national associations: Christian Leadership Alliance, Willow Creek Association (now Global Leadership Network), and Christian Camp and Conference Association. He is co-author, with former ECFA President Dan Busby of four books, including "Lessons from the Nonprofit Boardroom."

www.ingramcontent.com/pod-product-compliance
Lightning Source LLC
LaVergne TN
LVHW021342080426
835508LV00020B/2084